A GREAT AMERICAN COOK

A GREAT AMERICAN COOK

RECIPES FROM THE HOME KITCHEN OF ONE OF OUR MOST INFLUENTIAL CHEFS

JONATHAN WAXMAN

WITH TOM STEELE

FOREWORD BY BOBBY FLAY

PHOTOGRAPHS BY JOHN KERNICK

HOUGHTON MIFFLIN COMPANY

BOSTON   NEW YORK

2007

For information about permission to reproduce selections from
this book, write to Permissions, Houghton Mifflin Company,
215 Park Avenue South, New York, New York 10003.

Visit our Web site: www.houghtonmifflinbooks.com.

LIBRARY OF CONGRESS CATALOGING-IN-PUBLICATION DATA

Waxman, Jonathan.
A great American cook : recipes from the home kitchen
of one of our most influential chefs /
by Jonathan Waxman, with Tom Steele ; foreword by Bobby Flay ;
photographs by John Kernick.
p. cm.
Includes index.
ISBN-13: 978-0-618-65852-7
ISBN-10: 0-618-65852-1
1. Cookery, American.   2. Waxman, Jonathan.
3. Cookery, American—California style.
I. Steele, Tom.   II. Title.
TX715.W349 2007
641.5973—dc22   2007013975

Book design by Anne Chalmers
Food styling by Jee Levin
Prop styling by Denise Canter

Printed in China

C&C 10 9 8 7 6 5 4 3 2 1

TO MY WIFE, SALLY.

She has made me understand the value of family

and lovingly nudged me to realize that there

are other gifts in life besides food.

Those gifts are our three children,

HANNAH, ALEXANDER, AND FOSTER,

who have made my life complete.

ACKNOWLEDGMENTS

I often chide myself for not expressing my gratitude to the people who have been so crucial to my life as a chef. My mother, Adele, was my first instructor. Sadly, she hasn't seen the fruits of her efforts, but every time I cook, a little bit of her culinary DNA simmers inside me. My father, Arny, whose health has defied cigarettes and other vices, is still my biggest fan. I distinctly remember his Madeira-marinated hanger steak cooked in the living room fireplace. The aroma alone has served as a constant companion whenever I stand at a grill. My brothers, Rick and Michael, and their stalwart and amazing wives, Victoria and Tre, have stood at my emotional elbow, encouraging me at every juncture.

The importance of my discovering *The Joy of Cooking* can't be overstated. I don't know where that ragged copy (circa 1955) has gone, but for a long time, it was my culinary best friend. The recipes still resonate whenever I use flour, butter, and any other kitchen staple.

Julia Child also had a profound and gravitational effect on me. I was impressed by *Mastering the Art of French Cooking*, and her TV shows are indelibly etched in my cooking technique and, more important, in my cooking attitude.

I devoured many other early cooking shows. In particular, Graham Kerr delighted me with his offhanded approach and his straightforward advice. The ever-buoyant Mary Risely of Tante Marie's Cooking School pushed me to La Varenne in Paris. Had I gone another path, I might still be foundering.

My time in Paris was tumultuous, scary, hilarious, and fun. In Paris, the list of those I want to thank is lengthy, but most particularly, Chef Fernand Chambrette and Anne Willan. Gregory Usher and Robert Noah, who helped me find the impossible, a paying job in France, are no longer with us. And I owe a great debt to two eminent photographers, Chuck Baker and Dick Balarian (to whom I still owe $50, I think).

The chefs in Europe who have rocked my world include Michel Guérard, les frères Troisgros, les frères Haberlin, Gérard Boyer, and, most important, Frédy Girardet.

In America, the late wine doyen of Berkeley and old family friend Henry Rubin opened some doors and allowed me access to the kitchen at Domaine Chandon. There I met Philippe Jeanty, who at twenty was already a culinary wizard of grand standing. Udo Nechutnys taught me the valuable lessons of chef etiquette, humor, strength, and professionalism.

My greatest mentor in many ways has been Alice Waters. She hired me on the strength of my weird handwriting and tolerated me when I had no business being at Chez Panisse. She let me work with the brilliant Jean-Pierre Moullé. I also met my dear friend Mark Miller, who gave me a crash course in all things not French. And I came into contact with Deborah Madison, Judy Rodgers, and Lindsey Shere, who may be the best pastry chef I've ever encountered. Alice made it all happen.

I want to thank Michael McCarty for his guidance, vision, generosity, and sheer madness. Also my cooking partners at Michael's: Ken Frank, Mark Peel, Nancy Silverton, Gordon Naccarato, Martin Garcia, Kazuto Matsusaka, James Brinkley, and many more. My five years at the restaurant passed far too quickly: it was paradise.

I treasure my dear friend Sally Clarke, who I must thank for simply putting up with me.

From my days at Jams, I thank my partners Melvyn Master, Marvin Zeidler, and Larry Shupnick; André Soltner, for his kind words and inspiration; and Larry Forgione, for parting the waters, for making work fun, and for his kind, understanding friendship.

I also want to thank my current partners, Fabrizio Ferri, Philip Scotti, and Stephen Singer. Jeff Salaway, wherever you are, I miss eating and drinking with you. To Craig Schiffer, who, more than a fabulous friend, is my brother.

This book was a long time in coming. My sexy, extremely proficient agent, Jane Dystel, was my marathon companion, seeing this to fruition. Tom Steele, my most enthusiastic of muses, made my thoughts coalesce. My editor, Rux Martin, was neither timid nor shy in her vision. I needed a strong partner, and she was there at every juncture. Heartfelt thanks to Hunter Lewis, whose tireless and all-important testing of the recipes improved them for the home cook.

I am forever in debt to my copy editor, Judith Sutton. Without her, this book would not flow. Jacinta Monniere determinedly and steadily typed, checked, and rechecked all the myriad drafts and made for a smooth voyage. Anne Chalmers turned my food into art, with a fabulous and rich design. Michaela Sullivan transformed this old cook into the smiling guy on the cover.

As for the photography, my hat is off to the amazing John Kernick, who has a mercurial touch with lighting and a painter's eye for composition. Thanks to Jee Levin and Denise Canter for nailing the atmosphere. The photography is delicious.

—JONATHAN WAXMAN

I would like to thank dear Rebecca Bent, who first guided me to Jonathan Waxman; our diligent and brilliant editor, Rux Martin; and our assiduous agent, Jane Dystel. Jonathan has been an illuminating joy to work with every step of the way. I am also deeply grateful to my wondrous family and delicious friends, and in particular to Jonathan Bauchman, the new light of my life.

—TOM STEELE

CONTENTS

FOREWORD

by Bobby Flay

I'm often asked, "Who was your mentor?" The answer rolls off my tongue. It's Jonathan Waxman.

The mid-1980s brought the food revolution to America—and I was working for one of its generals. Going to work brought a new surprise every day—James Beard and Julia Child lunching in the dining room at Jonathan's New York restaurant Jams, munching on perfect French fries with mesquite-grilled chicken and polishing off a bottle of buttery American white wine. Or Wolfgang Puck and Alice Waters hanging out in the kitchen as they snacked on our prep work. It was intimidating, but it was the start of something special.

Like all great mentors, Jonathan had his own style of teaching and inspiring. It was not the old-school style of kitchen discipline that is so well documented, especially in European kitchens. No chef-as-tyrant, with pots and pans flying through the air or screaming at you in front of the rest of the staff because your vinaigrette was a touch too acidic. No, Jonathan taught through his respect of ingredients and his sensibility of techniques. He would rather reward you with a glass of Champagne at the end of a busy night or take you out for an after-service hamburger at J. G. Melon. It was so civilized, so productive, so exciting.

Jonathan was the first person to teach me what good food was. Until I went to work for him, I thought of cooking in a kitchen as more of a production than a craft. He taught more than the fundamentals; he taught how to layer flavors—flavors that are to this day the foundations of my food. He stressed the importance of salt and pepper and the subtle differences in oils that you cook with and oils that you don't. He guided me on when to use fresh goat cheese as opposed to aged, how long to cook mushrooms, and how to get the perfect crispiness on a chicken. He taught me how to dress a salad, respecting each tender green that landed on the plate. Jonathan used to say that the leaves should look like they had just fallen from the clouds, light and individual.

Jonathan employs certain ingredients to transform a usually bland dish into one bursting with flavor. His use of chile peppers and garlic, whether he's roasting them, sautéing them, or using them raw, is pure genius. He stirs some chipotle into mayonnaise for his deep-fried squid, sautés garlic and serrano chiles into his Mussel and Littleneck Clam Chowder, pairs poblano chiles with chicken breasts. With his touch, otherwise simple dishes become explosions of flavor.

Whenever I speak to fellow cooks who worked for Jonathan, there's always a moment when we mention to one another what a wonderful cook he is. We appreciate him now more than ever because we still use the techniques he taught us twenty years ago.

When Jonathan talks about great moments in his life, they usually revolve around a table filled with food. Over the years, I've heard him speak about eating a lobster roasted in a brick oven on the coast of Sicily and about jumping on a plane in New York to go have lunch at a Paris restaurant. But the best secret about Jonathan is his favorite snack. It's not caviar and crème fraîche or foie gras terrine with black truffles—no way. It's a fresh, slightly spicy guacamole with warm just-fried tortilla chips paired with an ice-cold margarita made with plenty of fresh lime juice.

In fact, the first thing Jonathan asked me to "cook" for him twenty years ago was a bowl of guacamole. Jonathan showed me how attention paid to each ingredient could make all the difference in the world. He explained how to mash the ripe avocados with a fork and fold in the aromatic ingredients such as chiles and onion so that the guacamole would have contrasting textures. He taught me to chop the cilantro coarsely to accentuate its freshness. He showed me that just a kiss of fresh lime juice brings all the flavors together. That was also the first time I fried my own corn tortillas to make chips. Jonathan told me that peanut oil would make them crisp and light. Jonathan's favorite snack might be mine now, too. Thankfully, he shares it with us on page 19.

When I worked for Jonathan, he would try to fry anything, from pumpkin to the perfect French fries. Deep-frying has taken some knocks in the media, but when done with diligence and with proper technique, it's hard to beat. Try his Fried Shrimp with Caper Mayonnaise and the aforementioned Deep-Fried Squid with Chipotle Mayonnaise; they'll become mainstays in your repertoire.

I'm honored to write the foreword to Jonathan's book for many reasons. For one, I can tell you the things that he won't. He is one of the fathers of New American cuisine, and he brought California-style cooking to the East Coast: introducing us to such ingredients as baby greens and baby vegetables, fresh and dried chile peppers, and blue corn; grilling on mesquite wood; cooking with Chardonnay; and saucing fish and meats with fresh salsas and relishes.

I'm happy to say that I first donned my whites as an aspiring cook in his kitchens at Buds and Jams, then at his French bistro Hulot's. Now when I need my Waxman fix, I tell the taxi driver to take me to Barbuto, in the West Village, for simple yet perfect Mediterranean cooking.

Now Jonathan, my number one mentor and one of the original practitioners of New American cuisine, finally shares his secrets with you in this long-awaited book.

A GREAT AMERICAN COOK

INTRODUCTION

For brevity's sake, I'm not going to recount my first moment with smoked salmon, and I'm not going to tell you that as a teenager I preferred reading Julia Child to playing baseball. I will say that food didn't always take first place in my heart. Music did. Originally I wanted to be a jazz trombonist, and as soon as I parted ways with home and education, I played every night from 11 p.m. to 6 a.m., then slept until noon and made myself a leisurely lunch.

With the onset of the disco era and a persistent notion that perhaps I didn't have enough musical talent, I began to think differently about my future. I was extremely reluctant to embrace anything resembling a suit-and-tie job, so my prospects were limited to bartending or selling cars. Somewhere along the line, though, as I was fooling around in the kitchen restoring myself for the night to come, I realized that I was enjoying cooking more than my music gigs.

I went to a cooking class at Macy's taught by Richard Grausman, the traveling chef of Cordon Bleu. I happened upon a new place in Berkeley called Chez Panisse and began spending more money than I earned eating there. I read every cookbook in the University of California's agricultural library. One fateful afternoon, I came across the *Juilliard Guide to France*, which described with relish the emerging cuisine. A friend suggested that I continue my culinary experiments at the school La Varenne in Paris. It was geared toward English-speaking students and took any rank amateur who could provide two requisites: money and time. My parents generously provided the necessary cash injection and on my twenty-sixth birthday, in 1976, I took off for Paris and the start of my cooking career.

The mid-1970s were a deliciously intoxicating time to be in France. At school I could hardly wait for each new recipe. At night I sampled as much food and wine as my limited budget would allow. The students were mostly American, and La Varenne's purpose was to teach us how to capture the French culinary magic and perpetuate it in America.

By the spring of 1977, I was having the time of my life. I was sharing an apartment with a couple of well-known fashion photographers and three models. I had a little money and four willing student accomplices, so we decided to conquer the three-star joints of France. In a broken-down Opel with a two-by-four holding up the front seat, we began touring the country. On a wintry Sunday night, we pulled up to our first three-star restaurant, the remarkable Frères Troisgros, intrepid but very nervous. We were treated like royalty. The meal surpassed anything I'd ever experienced by light-years.

The next day dawned, and one member of our group, having fêted a bit excessively, left us and returned to Paris. We survivors decided that the weather was too blustery to carry on that day, so we went into the bar of Frères Troisgros to have a drink. Jean Troisgros, the taller, more patrician brother, looked us over and asked, "Would you care for a snack?" After polishing off a panoply of fish, a gigantic côte de boeuf, and a sensuous chocolate dessert along with two carafes of Fleurie, we were converted into disciples of *nouvelle cuisine aux Troisgros*. What I remember most about this extraordinary experience was the passion of the cooks in the kitchen. They seemed to be in a kind of rapture: calm, dedicated, and totally fearless. It reminded me of the great musicians I'd seen.

From that moment on, I was determined to acquire as much skill and experience as it would take to translate what the Troisgros brothers had accomplished into an American idiom. Food at home had grown timid, conservative, and, on the whole, boring. These Frenchmen had used their classical training to break the rules, and, above all, they had learned to improvise. How fantastic!

My desire to develop my own culinary voice was also stimulated by the growing number of chefs elsewhere in France, who, like the Troisgros brothers, were intent on pushing aside the stodgy old rules. The term "seasonal" was becoming as important as any kitchen tool. "Regional" and "fresh" too had new gustatory status. The cuisines of Japan, Spain, Italy, China, Thailand, and, yes, even America became sources for inspiration.

As my stay in Paris came to an end, I found I was not anxious to get home. Instead, I got an apprenticeship in the Vosges region near the Swiss border at a little Relais Châteaux inn. I cooked everything there, from mayonnaise to génoise, from terrine de canard to pheasant à la royale, working 8 a.m. to 1 a.m. seven days a week. The chef was tolerant, the owner overworked, the guests blissfully removed from my life. I slept in a farmhouse more suitable for raising pigs than sheltering cooks. I lost twenty pounds, gained considerable knowledge and experience, and obtained a coveted *carte du travail,* allowing one to work there legally.

My jazz career had prepared me for chefdom in one small way: I quickly learned that practice and repetition are the most important aspects of a culinary life. Jazz had also bred in me some talent for improvisation, and I began to reread and question the classic dishes.

Fate intervened when my father summoned me home to care for my ailing mother. I quickly found work at Domaine Chandon's fledgling winery in Napa, and then, after a fairly disastrous stint in Monterey, where I discovered that I knew only about 15 percent of the necessary skills, I landed back at Chez Panisse with Alice Waters, this time in the kitchen. Alice believes that none of us should ever take any of what we cook for granted. Emotions, passion, integrity, and thoughtfulness are all essential to good food. If we can instruct and nourish through our cooking skills and do it with a sense of fun and caring, perhaps we can bring about a modicum of spiritual contentment.

Armed with these heady ideas, I was off to Los Angeles and Michael's restaurant, which by that time had acquired a burgeoning international reputation. We were determined to marry the philosophy of the French with an American sensibility. In those wild, experimental days, no recipe was written in stone. Our culinary synthesis of ingredient-focused cooking, charcoal grilling, and lighter sauces became the basis for what many referred to as "California cuisine." A demand for freshness, be it seafood, poultry, or lettuces, was our first order of the day. Our suppliers, unfortunately, were clueless, but the growers themselves rose to the occasion. Soon we had real vegetables, wonderfully diverse garden greens, great quail, and spring lamb coming to the back door of our kitchen every day. Michael's enthusiasm and confidence in my abilities transformed me. I had been a stumbling, timid cook, and I became a confident and secure chef. My judgment still sometimes suffered from overenthusiasm, but in the main, my technique had finally caught up with my imagination.

The next step was logical: my own joint. With the launch of Jams in New York City in 1984, California came east. New Yorkers at that time had no use for charcoal grills. They used them occasionally for summer barbecues in the Hamptons, but no restaurant of note had a charcoal grill on the premises. Most places relied on a gas "grill" that basically burned food rather than imparting that wonderful smoky crispness. But when Jams opened, my promised stoves had still not arrived. I purchased two Weber grills, and they also served as my ovens and sauté stations. After another week passed, I used a makeshift grill made by a Chinese craftsman, and that had to do until I had enough money to buy a Montague, a beautiful grill from Hayward, California, modeled after one from Maxim's in Paris, circa 1930. That grill enabled me to cook a split chicken in 20 minutes. The food, colorful, tasty, and vibrant, with the aroma of mesquite charcoal and intensely flavored sauces, worked a certain magic on New Yorkers. The influence of East Coast ingredients, like soft-shell crabs, white corn, and Maine lobster, propelled my cooking to a new dimension.

But the true turning point in my becoming a well-rounded cook was marriage. From the outset, my wife knew there was some taming to be accomplished. I took time off and cooked for her at home. The dishes I made bore little resemblance to those I served in my restaurant. I was content to visit the market and pick up some clams, oregano, sweet butter, and whole wheat pasta for dinner. With no time restraints or the need to be fancy, my cooking slowly became more homey and rustic. My muse had shifted, and my inner homebody took over. A bunch of asparagus bought from a farmer with the dirt still clinging was a special event.

The recipes in this book range from the simple to the elaborate. They encourage you to flex your culinary muscles with a flourish. The best advice I can give is to practice, practice, practice. Don't let yourself feel intimidated by a lack of experience. Take the plunge, and your skills will hone themselves.

How do you cook a meal that will thrill the most jaded palate? I hope these recipes will shed some light.

EDICTS ON SELECTED INGREDIENTS AND TECHNIQUES

Before I begin, I'd like to issue some culinary edicts from on high. I'll try not to pontificate, but I really do feel pretty strongly about most of the following.

BACON

OK, I love bacon (and, yeah, I'm from a Jewish household). We're in luck these days: bacon with no nitrates, nitrites, or other additives is widely available. I prefer slab bacon, but if you can't get that, use thick-sliced country-smoked bacon with no sugar added. Nueske, Niman Ranch, and Applegate are all great.

BOUQUET GARNI

A marvelous flavoring agent for stocks, sauces, and stews, a bouquet garni is an herb bundle that combines bay leaves, parsley sprigs, leek greens, ginger, and black peppercorns, tied up in a cheesecloth sack. You can forget the cheesecloth if you're in a hurry. Just throw the herbs and spices in; fishing them out later is not usually much of a problem.

BUTTER

There's a lot of butter flowing through these recipes. Always use unsalted butter, for two reasons: you can control the salt levels in a dish yourself, and unsalted butter is usually fresher—salt obscures the rancid taste that can ruin a dish. When I call for butter, I mean unsalted, organic, preferably freshly churned butter with low water content.

In times past, various techniques were used to churn cream, and the liquid (buttermilk) and the solid fat (butter) were then separated. Butter made in this fashion is now sold as "cultured butter," as distinguished from the more common "sweet butter," which is made from unfermented milk.

I prefer cultured butter, which has a richer flavor. The best organic cultured butter I've found is made by Vermont Butter & Cheese. It's dense and very yellow, and it enriches sauces beautifully. Of the national brands, Land O'Lakes organic and Horizon are fine, but if you can find a local creamery, try their butter. It may be a revelation.

COOKWARE

Men do like their toys, especially pots, pans, and knives. I am very fond of heavy maple chopping blocks, German spatulas, Swiss kitchen gadgets, French casseroles, and Belgian copperware. Here are some of my favorites.

Stainless steel are the best all-around pots and pans. They are lighter than copper, do not react with acid ingredients, and are good for all kinds of cooking. Food can stick if they are not well made, and they're a bit difficult to clean if heavily soiled. A widely available fine-grade cleansing powder called Bar Keeper's Friend and a stainless steel pad will do the trick.

American cast-iron skillets and Dutch ovens mellow with age, are good heat conductors, and are excellent for searing, stewing, braising, oven-roasting, and more. They do react with acidic ingredients such as citrus fruit, wine, and tomatoes, so avoid cooking anything in which acidic ingredients are primary.

Le Creuset enameled cast-iron cookware is my favorite. These pots and skillets are superior heat conductors, take on a delightful patina with use, and are noncorrosive, nonreactive, and virtually indestructible. They look good on the table, and they retain heat admirably. There are other similar brands, but Le Creuset is the benchmark.

Copper pans are superior heat conductors. Although they are heavy and difficult to keep spotless, they'll last five lifetimes. Because copper is reactive, I use heavy-gauge copper lined with stainless steel. The drawbacks are that these copper pans are quite expensive and food tends to stick to the stainless steel interior if it's not properly cared for.

Avoid nonstick pans! They don't distribute heat properly, it's nearly impossible to sear in them, and the nonstick element can start to shed into your food. If you must buy one, choose the most expensive one and read the directions carefully.

CRABMEAT

Alaskan king crabs are truly a wonder of the sea. Even frozen, the meat is exquisite. Maryland blue crabs are found along the entire Atlantic and Gulf Coast. Fresh from a good supplier, the meat is heaven, but frozen, it can be watery and flavorless. Stone crab claws are dense and prodigiously flavorful. Dungeness, hailing from the Pacific, are available mostly locally and in season in the winter. Other local crabs include peekytoe from Maine and Jonah from the coasts of California and Oregon. If possible, taste crabmeat before buying: taste and freshness are paramount.

FLOUR

While old-fashioned national brands like Gold Medal are fine, you'll notice a marked difference between a mass-produced bleached product and, say, King Arthur organic flour. Here are the types I use.

Stone-ground, unbleached, organic all-purpose flour
Stone-ground, unbleached, organic bread flour
Stone-ground, unbleached, organic pastry flour

FOOD TEMPERATURES

As a general rule of thumb, all foods need to "temper," or gradually come up to a suitable temperature, for proper cooking. There are many variations on this theme, including the following.

Poultry should sit at room temperature for 1 hour before cooking.
Lamb, beef, and pork should be at 60 degrees before cooking, never colder, or the meat will cook unevenly, with the center undercooked.

Fish can generally be left in the refrigerator until just before cooking, to keep it from spoiling, but it should not be too cold.

Generally, vegetables should be at room temperature before cooking to avoid uneven cooking.

When making bread doughs, have all the ingredients except the water at 72 to 90 degrees. Temperature variance will affect the way the dough comes together and rises.

Likewise, when making pastry, have all the ingredients and utensils cool or cold to the touch.

GARLIC

My training in France and at Chez Panisse regarding the preparation of garlic was strict: always remove the green stem from the center of mature cloves. If you can, buy immature garlic or very fresh new garlic, so fresh that the skin hasn't time to toughen. Second trick: tap the cloves with the side of a heavy knife. The skins will pop off. To smash garlic, cut the cloves in half and, holding the side of the knife firmly against the rounded side of the cloves, whack them with your fist. You'll end up with a beautiful teaspoon of smashed garlic. Burned garlic is no good—always cook it gently.

GRILLING

I've spent more than thirty years cooking on a grill. Here are some tricks.

Use good hardwood charcoal.

Clean the grill grid and intake vents. A clean grill is a happy one.

Start the grill 45 minutes ahead so the coals are at their optimum.

Make sure you use enough charcoal; in some cases, you may need to replenish the charcoal.

Have your tongs, grill brush, spatula, and all your serving platters at the ready.

Have all the cooking ingredients, including salt, pepper, and olive oil, ready on a table nearby.

A glass of good wine is essential.

Grilling has three levels of heat: medium-high, the level where the coals have just died down and they are white but still very hot; medium, when you can keep your open hand over the grill for at least 10 seconds; and low, when the grill has cooled way down.

I use a Weber grill. This marvelous piece of equipment can accomplish a number of things: If the fire is too hot, you can cover it with the dome and reduce air circulation with the top vents. Or if you want indirect heat, just shove the coals to one side.

KNIVES

For years at Michael's and Jams, a Wüsthof standard stainless steel knife with a 10-inch blade was my right hand. Lately, I've become enamored with some Japanese knives. I use about the same size knife, but it is made of Japanese steel, with very small amounts of chrome. It's a bit harder to keep clean, but the sharpness is unparalleled. It also stays sharp longer. I buy it from Korin in Manhattan, but you can find versions at other stores, including Williams-Sonoma and Bed Bath & Beyond.

OIL

For frying, I like peanut or corn oil. I am not a fan of canola oil, which I think has a weird taste. I use regular olive oil for shallow-frying. For cooking and sauces, I like a softer olive oil, such as one from Spain or the South of France. Oil from Pantelleria in Sicily is particularly versatile. I prefer pungent, spicier green Tuscan oils for dressings and vinaigrettes, or for brushing on grilled toasted bread rubbed with garlic.

I also love toasted walnut and hazelnut oils from Switzerland and the mountains of France. Keep in mind that these oils are especially perishable and can go rancid quickly; I buy them in small bottles so as not to run the risk of spoilage and forgo that fantastic bargain at Costco.

ONIONS

Use sweet onions raw, in tarts, and for quick sautéing or roasting. The more mature storage onions, yellow, white, and red, are better for stews, stocks, and other hearty dishes. Regionally America is blessed with sweet Vidalia onions from Georgia (which have two seasons, late spring and October); Mauis (a good reason to visit Hawaii);

Texas Sweets, which are huge; Stockton Reds, from the Sacramento River Delta; and Walla Wallas, from Washington State.

ORGANIC INGREDIENTS

You'd expect a Berkeley, California, boy to identify strongly with the sustainable agriculture philosophy, and I guess I was radical in my sociopolitical perspective when I was younger, but the roots of my organic product obsession actually began much earlier. My grandparents were organic farmers by necessity. Pesticides and DDT were widely used in the 1950s, but they were too costly and time-consuming for small farms. Nonorganic substances were minimally applied. Thus, I discovered on my own how completely different an organic apple was from a store-bought variety. An animal is far happier scooting around a field or a pond rather than stuck in a cage or an artificially lighted barn.

Sustainable products are superior in both flavor and nutrition. But there are certain caveats: Some so-called organic products are shams, or, worse, they start off as gorgeous field-fresh products, only to languish sadly in warehouses, without proper handling or temperature. Then they're foisted off at high prices to gullible consumers. Make sure what you buy is fresh.

POULTRY

I'm the grandson of a poultry farmer, so my passion for perfect birds is extreme. Many people ask me what we use at the restaurant. I try to use free-range, organic, corn-fed (again organic), air-dried poultry.

SALMON

I recommend wild salmon, regardless of cost. Some extraordinary salmon are fished off the coast of Alaska in the early summer: try the magnificent kings. Farmed salmon don't look or feel right: the fins aren't well developed, and the flesh is flabby and less flavorful.

SALT

My grandmother would have said, "Salt is salt." But salt is not all the same. I love sea salt. There are many varieties. I like Maldon salt from England or sel gris from Brittany. For an everyday salt, I recommend kosher. It comes in one grade, medium-coarse, which lends itself to many uses. For final seasoning, I use sea salt.

SPICES

Spices are the most underappreciated ingredients in the modern kitchen. Consider that long and serious wars were fought over spices! I love nutmeg and cinnamon, and they work well in savory dishes as well as desserts. I appreciate true paprika from Hungary, and I have a soft spot for saffron from La Mancha—which is the most expensive ingredient of all pound for pound, because it must be harvested entirely by hand. Some spices are fine out of the bottle, but all spices have a shelf life. Two-year-old ground cinnamon is a pale version of its freshly bottled self. I recommend replacing any ground spice once a year. I prefer freshly grated whole nutmeg to preground, but I understand that expediency sometimes has its place.

STOVES

A good cook should be able to cook anything, anywhere, on anything. You should be able to make a great meal with a Bunsen burner and a cast-iron skillet, or a hibachi and a bag of charcoal. That said, gas is better than electric. If you are in the market for a new stove, my advice is to ask your cooking friends what they like and dislike about their ranges, then ask if you can take one for a test-drive. Cooking on my cobalt-blue Viking, which has a grill and a convection oven, is like driving a Bentley.

STARTERS

GUESTS REMEMBER STARTERS
MORE VIVIDLY THAN
ANY OTHER COURSE.

Guests remember starters more vividly than any other course. A memorable meal should begin by establishing a pace and/or a theme to tantalize your guests. The appetizer might be a bit frivolous, perhaps not as serious as the main course you choose. My red pepper pancakes, for instance, are at once unusual, extravagant, and fun. My favorite starters often have a twist—a contrast between hot and cold or crunchy and soft—as well as a juxtaposition of flavors.

Hot appetizers like Deep-Fried Squid with Chipotle Mayonnaise will jump-start a meal with a flourish, but sometimes the simplest of appetizers can be the greatest crowd-pleasers of all. Oysters grilled or heated under the broiler and served with sizzling black pepper butter evoke as much enthusiasm as any other dish I've created. All of these starters convey a strong sense of a light and free spirit.

STARTERS

RED PEPPER PANCAKES WITH CORN AND CAVIAR

8 pancakes, serving 4

When I worked in the kitchen at Chez Panisse, in the late 1970s, preparation was typically chaotic and impossible to accomplish in a normal twelve-hour working day. Because the menu changed so often and ingredients might or might not pan out, we were often behind the proverbial eight ball, dashing to complete the next day's *mise en place* after service each evening. One long night, we found ourselves particularly behind, so much so that when at 11:30 p.m., Alice Waters asked who had butchered the lamb for the next day's menu, we all groaned and looked at each other.

"Well," said Alice, "Jonathan, how about it?" And before I could utter a word of defiance or plead exhaustion, she turned away and grabbed a buckwheat blini, spooned a bit of crème fraîche on it, and proceeded to heap a good four ounces of beluga caviar on top. She shoved it into my hand, smiled, and, as the caviar dripped down my arm, asked sweetly, "Need another?"

I succumbed, and I finished the lamb in the wee hours of the morning. The blini were wonderful, to say nothing of the caviar, and I was inspired to rethink this Russian classic. The idea of coupling a savory red pepper pancake with a corn sauce seemed like a natural. Adding a small amount of smoked salmon and chives, as well as caviar, also seemed to fit. The pancakes proved to be a smash hit, and while somewhat labor-intensive, to say nothing of expensive, they are truly elegant and will make any special occasion more special.

I've often served these pancakes at room temperature.

2 medium red bell peppers

3 large eggs

3 tablespoons unsalted butter

1 tablespoon plus a squeeze of fresh lemon juice

½ cup all-purpose flour

Kosher salt

1 teaspoon baking powder

1 tablespoon minced fresh chives

½ cup crème fraîche

4 ounces sliced smoked salmon

2 ears corn, shucked, kernels cut off with a sharp knife

½ cup heavy cream

Butter or olive oil for frying the pancakes

1–2 ounces American caviar: paddlefish, salmon, or whitefish

½ cup small fresh cilantro sprigs

Roast the peppers over medium-high heat on the stovetop or under a hot broiler, turning occasionally, until blackened and blistered on all sides. Place the peppers in a bowl, cover with plastic wrap, and let them steam for 15 minutes.

Peel the peppers with your fingers (do not rinse) and stem and seed them.

Finely dice 1 of the peppers and set aside. Puree the remaining pepper in a blender or processor. Separate the eggs. Add the egg yolks to the pepper puree, blend well, and pour into a small bowl. Melt 2 tablespoons of the butter and let cool slightly, then stir it into the pepper puree. Add the tablespoon of lemon juice and whisk well.

Sift the flour into a medium bowl, add a pinch of salt and the baking powder, and stir in the pepper puree. With an electric mixer, in a medium bowl, beat the egg whites to soft peaks. Fold about one fourth of the whites into the flour-pepper mixture, then fold in all the remaining whites. Let the batter sit for 30 minutes at room temperature, or cover and refrigerate overnight; bring to room temperature before proceeding.

Fold the minced chives into the crème fraîche. Cut the sliced salmon into thin strips.

Melt the remaining 1 tablespoon butter in a medium skillet. Add the corn and sauté for about 2 minutes. Stir in the cream and the diced pepper, then add the squeeze of lemon juice. Remove from the heat and keep warm.

Just before serving, heat 1 to 2 tablespoons butter or olive oil in a large skillet over medium heat. Pour in about 1 tablespoon batter for each pancake, to make 2½- to 3-inch pancakes. Cook the pancakes in batches until they've lightly browned on the first side, about 1 minute, then turn and cook for about 1 minute on the second side, adding more butter or oil as necessary to fry the remaining pancakes.

Place 2 pancakes on each of four plates. Top each one with a dollop of crème fraîche. Arrange a few salmon strips on each pancake, coiling them loosely. Place a small dollop of caviar on top of each pancake. Spoon the corn sauce around the pancakes and garnish with the cilantro.

GUACAMOLE AND FRESH CHIPS
6 servings

To this day, my first choice for a comfort meal is home-cooked corn tortillas, a freshly made tub of guacamole, and a margarita. My version of guacamole is partly based on that of one of my Mexican buddies, Carolynn Carreño, who learned it from her grandmother.

A fruit that is treated like a vegetable, the avocado is comforting—creamy and satisfying. It is also one of the most versatile of foods. Mexicans use avocados in soups, salads, and entrées, even in desserts. Avocados are very delicate. A properly ripe avocado bruises easily, and once bruised, it will look green for just a few minutes, then brown. Hand mashing with a fork is the proper technique, and it reduces the flesh to a creamy, chunky mass that easily accepts the flavorings.

4 cups corn oil or peanut oil	1 cup chopped fresh cilantro
12 slightly stale corn tortillas	1 teaspoon kosher salt, or more to taste
Sea salt	4 ripe Hass avocados
½ sweet onion, such as Vidalia	1 lemon
2 jalapeño chiles	1 lime
1 serrano chile	

Heat the oil in a deep heavy skillet to 350 degrees. Meanwhile, cut the tortillas into eighths (wedges) or into 1-inch strips. Cook the chips, in 3 batches, until medium golden in color. Do not undercook! Remove the chips from the oil with a slotted spoon to paper towels to drain, and immediately sprinkle them with sea salt.

Finely mince the onion. Remove the stems and seeds from the chiles. Place the onion, chiles, cilantro, and kosher salt in a molcajete or mortar and pestle or a small food processor and mash or puree until almost liquid. Peel and pit the avocados, place them in a medium bowl, and mash them well with a fork. Fold in the onion mixture. Juice the lemon and lime and stir as much of the juice as you like into the guacamole. Taste for salt and add more if needed.

Transfer the guacamole to a serving bowl and serve with the chips.

SHIITAKE MUSHROOM SPRING ROLLS

About 30 rolls

I once owned a wonderful restaurant in Napa Valley called Table 29. During construction, I had mentioned to the folks at Silverado Vineyards that I loved olive trees. One day, they called me out of the blue and asked if by any chance I needed a few extra trees. Well, as a matter of fact, I'd already talked to some horticultural people about buying some. The Silverado trees were about 100 years old, and I could have as many as I liked. "How much?" I asked. "Free," they replied. "Just arrange for their transportation, and they're yours." That was generosity beyond all generosity.

A few months later, the vineyard owners asked if I ever did catering. "All the time," I responded. Their tenth anniversary party turned out to be quite a spectacular affair. The hors d'oeuvres included these crisp baked spring rolls. They were a great hit.

1 leek	1 lime
2 large carrots	1 cup shredded napa cabbage
1 white onion	1 cup mung bean sprouts
1 jalapeño chile	¼ cup soy sauce
4 garlic cloves	1 tablespoon minced peeled fresh ginger
1 pound shiitake mushrooms	or preserved ginger
¼ cup olive oil, plus more for brushing the rolls	About 30 square wonton wrappers (about ½ package)
1 tablespoon toasted sesame oil	
Kosher salt and freshly ground black pepper	

Wash and trim the leek, and cut into julienne. Julienne the carrots, onion, and chile, keeping the chile separate. Sliver the garlic. Stem the shiitakes and slice the caps into julienne.

In a large skillet, heat the olive oil and sesame oil over medium heat. Add the leek, carrots, onion, and garlic, season with salt and pepper, and cook for 3 minutes. Add the mushrooms, chile, and ¼ cup water and cook for 10 minutes, or until the water evaporates.

Juice the lime. Add the cabbage and bean sprouts to the skillet, then add the lime juice, soy sauce, and ginger and mix well. Remove from the heat, cover, and let steam for a few minutes. Remove the cover and let cool.

Heat the oven to 400 degrees.

To assemble the spring rolls, place a wonton wrapper on a work surface with a point toward you. Moisten the edges of the wrapper with water and place 1 tablespoon of the shiitake mixture in the center. Fold the top corner over the filling, forming a plump triangle, and press the edges to seal, dipping your fingertips in a little water if necessary. Repeat until you have used all the filling.

With a pastry brush, paint the top of each roll with a little olive oil, and place on a baking sheet. Bake for 20 to 30 minutes, or until golden and crispy. Serve hot.

WARM SWEET ONION TART

6 servings

The onion tarts I encountered everywhere in Alsace—served in slivers as an appetizer or for lunch—were light, tasty, and delicious. I wanted to create a version as light as the ones I'd tasted, but in fact mine is even lighter and fluffier than its Alsatian predecessors, and it uses fewer eggs and less cream. The trick is to extract as much liquid from the onions as possible and then intensify their flavor by caramelizing them. Despite the fact that the filling has just seven ingredients, the tart tastes complex. You don't even need to make a dough, since it uses store-bought puff pastry.

2 large sweet onions, such as Vidalia
4 tablespoons (½ stick) unsalted butter
½ cup balsamic vinegar
 Kosher salt and freshly ground
  black pepper
½ pound puff pastry, preferably an
  all-butter brand such as Dufour
  (or 1 sheet pastry from a
  17 ¼-ounce package)

2 large eggs
½ cup heavy cream
 A few thyme blossoms
  or 1 teaspoon fresh thyme leaves

Slice the onions crosswise as thin as possible. Place a large skillet over very low heat. Add the butter and when it melts, stir in the onions. Cook, stirring occasionally, for 30 minutes, or until the onions are very soft and deep golden brown.

Add the vinegar to the onions and cook until it has reduced and slightly thickened, 5 to 10 minutes. Remove from the heat and let cool, then season with salt and pepper.

Heat the oven to 400 degrees.

On a lightly floured surface, roll out the puff pastry ¼ inch thick. Using a pot lid or a plate as a guide, cut the pastry into a 10-inch round. Fit the pastry into an 8-inch tart pan with a removable bottom. Trim the edges of the pastry if necessary and prick it all over with a fork. Bake for 15 to 20 minutes, or until golden brown on the bottom. (Don't be afraid that the tart shell will burn later when it is baked again—the filling will prevent that from happening.) Take the tart shell out of the oven and let cool on a rack for 10 minutes.

Whisk the eggs lightly in a medium bowl. Add the cream and thyme and blend well, then season with salt and pepper. Spread the onions evenly in the tart shell. Pour the egg mixture over the onions and stir gently with a fork so the custard mixture spreads evenly in the tart shell.

Bake the tart for 25 minutes, or until just set. Remove and let cool on a rack. Serve warm or at room temperature, cut into wedges.

ASPARAGUS WITH ORANGES AND HAZELNUTS

6 to 8 servings

It wasn't until I arrived in Paris and someone told me that asparagus was not seen until early spring and sometimes not until late April that I realized that it is supposed to be a seasonal vegetable. And to my amazement, the big white or purple beauties that appeared then weren't at all like the bland asparagus to which I had been accustomed in California year-round. The European varieties boasted soft, rounded tips and thick, stalky bodies that required peeling, and they were the best that I had ever tasted. On returning to America, I found that we, too, grow wonderfully fat asparagus in certain areas. It's always best if you buy it from a local grower (or grow it yourself).

3 pounds large white, green, or purple asparagus	1 tablespoon toasted sesame oil
3 Cara Cara or other seedless oranges	1 cup hazelnuts
¼ cup good extra-virgin olive oil	Sea salt and freshly ground black pepper

Heat the oven to 400 degrees.

Holding a spear of asparagus by its tip and its tail, bring the ends together: the bottom will snap off at the point where its bitterness ends. Trim the rest of the asparagus to approximately the same length.

Fill a large pot or deep skillet with salted water and bring to a boil. Meanwhile, peel the oranges and cut them into slices. In a medium bowl, toss the orange slices with both oils.

Spread the hazelnuts on a rimmed baking sheet and toast in the oven, stirring occasionally, for 10 minutes.

Meanwhile, place the asparagus in the boiling water. The cooking time will vary depending on the size of the asparagus, but start testing it 4 minutes after the water has returned to a boil. When the asparagus is crisp-tender, drain it well, then drain on a kitchen towel. Arrange the asparagus on plates.

Lightly crush the hazelnuts. Season the oranges with salt and pepper and toss with the hazelnuts. Spoon over the asparagus and serve immediately.

POTATO SKINS WITH POTATO SALAD

4 servings

Potato skins, a staple of my early diet, are the basis of this rustic yet elegant dish. The skins are crunchy and filled with a delectably tart potato salad and are served on coleslaw. This whimsical recipe evokes both my childhood and my vision of modern American food.

4	medium russet potatoes, 12–14 ounces each
2	tablespoons corn oil or peanut oil
	Kosher salt and freshly ground black pepper
1	bunch scallions

1	garlic clove
2	tablespoons sherry vinegar
⅓	cup plus 2 tablespoons olive oil
¼	cup red wine vinegar
1	medium red cabbage, cored and shredded

Heat the oven to 450 degrees.

Wash the potatoes and prick them all over with a fork. Place them directly on an oven rack and roast for 45 minutes, or until tender. Remove the potatoes from the oven and let them cool for 15 minutes. Leave the oven on.

Cut the potatoes lengthwise in half. Scoop out all the pulp and place it in a large bowl.

Toss the potato skins with the corn or peanut oil, season with salt and pepper, and place skin side down on a baking sheet. Bake until golden brown, about 15 minutes.

Meanwhile, finely mince the scallions and garlic. Stir them into the bowl of potatoes, add the sherry vinegar and ⅓ cup of the olive oil, and mix well, but don't make a puree—leave the potatoes chunky.

Stuff the warm potato skins with the potato salad.

In a large bowl, whisk the red wine vinegar with the remaining 2 tablespoons olive oil. Add the cabbage, season with salt and pepper, and toss well.

Place the cabbage on a platter and top with the stuffed potato skins.

APPLE AND CHICKEN LIVER MOUSSE

10 to 15 servings

I visited Georges Blanc, an unpretentious riverside restaurant in Vonnas, a small town in southern Burgundy, just days after the Michelin guide had elevated the establishment to three-star status. The place was understandably in a state of excitement. I fell in love with a chicken mousseline I had that night. Blanc had transformed a simple chicken mousse into a truly ethereal concoction. The main ingredient was perfect blond livers from prized Bresse chickens, which were raised a stone's throw from the restaurant.

I knew that our chickens were not capable of producing those huge pale livers, but I thought perhaps I could do something else to achieve a similar great-tasting dish. I began by coating livers generously with sea salt and black pepper, then pan-seared them in olive oil at a high temperature. When they were dark brown on the outside but still rare inside, I removed them and added some diced apples to the hot skillet: they caramelized instantly. I poured in Calvados, cognac, and cream. Finally, I pureed the cooled livers and apples with toasted walnuts. The last ingredient is all-important: a good dose of sweet butter. While the result, served with toasted walnut bread, does not taste exactly like Blanc's mousse, it has its own charm.

2 pounds fresh chicken livers,
    preferably organic, trimmed
Sea salt and freshly ground
    black pepper
1 pound baking apples, such as
    Rome Beauty or Gala
4 shallots
1 cup walnuts

¼ cup olive oil
¼ cup Calvados or bourbon
¼ cup cognac
1 cup heavy cream
8 tablespoons (1 stick) unsalted butter
    Toasted slices of walnut bread or good
        pumpernickel or white country bread

Heat the oven to 350 degrees.

Liberally coat the livers with sea salt and pepper; set aside on a plate. Peel and core the apples and cut into ¼-inch dice. Chop the shallots.

Spread the walnuts on a baking sheet and lightly toast in the oven, 5 to 8 minutes, stirring occasionally. Transfer to a plate.

In a large heavy enameled or other nonreactive skillet, heat the oil until it almost begins to smoke. Add the livers and stir them rapidly to sear, then cook for about 4 minutes, turning once. Remove the livers to a plate just when they become mahogany colored.

Add the apples and shallots to the skillet and cook for 5 minutes, or until softened. Turn off the heat, and carefully pour in the Calvados and cognac. Stir in the cream.

Melt the butter and let cool.

Combine the livers, apple mixture, and walnuts in a blender and puree just until the mixture is homogenous. Add the melted butter and blend well, then season to taste with salt and pepper. If you want the mousse to be very smooth, pass it through a fine-mesh sieve. Taste again for salt and pepper, transfer to a ceramic crock, cover with plastic wrap, and refrigerate for up to 2 days.

Serve with the walnut toast.

DUCK LIVER AND POTATO SALAD
WITH CHILE VINAIGRETTE

4 to 6 servings

Duck livers hold a special place for me. This wintry salad, with chestnuts, mâche (sometimes called lamb's tongue), frisée, and chiles, perfectly showcases the mellow, rich flavor of the livers. The salad was inspired by a meal long ago at the three-star restaurant Boyer near Epernay in France's Champagne region. Serve with amontillado sherry.

Duck livers are available from specialty butchers.

¾ pound fresh duck livers or chicken livers	**Vinaigrette**
Milk	1 poblano or Anaheim chile
1 tablespoon sea salt	¼ cup sherry vinegar
1½ teaspoons cracked black pepper	½ cup extra-virgin olive oil
½ pound fingerling or Yellow Finn potatoes	Sea salt and freshly ground black pepper
½ pound fresh chestnuts	2 tablespoons unsalted butter
2 tablespoons toasted sesame oil	1 small white onion
1 bunch mâche	2 jarred pimientos
1 bunch frisée	1 tablespoon olive oil

Soak the livers in milk to cover for at least 1 hour, or overnight. Drain and pat dry.

Heat the oven to 425 degrees.

Leave the livers whole or separate them into lobes. Sprinkle with the sea salt and pepper, then place on a plate, cover, and refrigerate.

Fill a medium bowl with ice water. Peel the potatoes and cut them into ¹⁄₁₆-inch-thick coins, placing the slices in the ice water as you work.

Make a cross in the flat side of each chestnut with a paring knife. Place them on a baking sheet and roast for 15 minutes, or until the cut edges of the shells begin to curl. While the chestnuts are still warm, peel them using a paring knife. Peel off the light-colored inner skins as well.

Place the chestnuts in a small bowl and toss with the sesame oil. Spread them on a baking sheet and roast, stirring occasionally, until toasted and golden, about 15 minutes. Let cool slightly, then coarsely chop.

Keeping the little bunches intact, wash the mâche and frisée. Dry thoroughly. Refrigerate until ready to serve.

MAKE THE VINAIGRETTE

Seed the chile and dice it very fine. Place it in a small bowl with the vinegar, then whisk in the olive oil and salt and pepper to taste. Set aside.

Drain the potatoes and pat them dry with paper towels. Melt the butter in a large skillet over medium heat. Add the potatoes to the skillet in a single layer and cook until golden brown and crisp on the first side, about 12 minutes. Turn the potatoes and cook until golden brown and crisp on the second side, 10 to 12 minutes.

Meanwhile, dice the onion and the pimientos, keeping them separate.

When the potatoes are cooked, transfer them to a large bowl. Add the onion to the skillet and cook, stirring, until softened. Remove from the heat.

Heat the olive oil in a large cast-iron or other heavy skillet over medium-high heat. When the skillet is hot, add the livers. Cook, turning once, until crisp outside but still rare inside, about 1 minute per side. Immediately transfer to a plate.

Add the greens, onion, pimientos, chestnuts, and vinaigrette to the potatoes and toss well. Spread on a platter, arrange the livers on top, and serve.

MUSHROOM AND TOMATO RAGOUT

6 servings

In this simple ragout, the crunchy toasts soak up all the good juices of mushrooms, tomatoes, and diced asparagus flavored with fresh herbs. For just half an hour or less of preparation, you'll get a deeply delicious result.

1 pound chanterelle or cremini mushrooms	1 poblano chile
3 shallots	½ pound asparagus, preferably white
2 large beefsteak tomatoes or 4 plum tomatoes	6 tablespoons (¾ stick) unsalted butter
6 ½-inch-thick slices white country bread	2 tablespoons Madeira wine
1 large garlic clove	1 teaspoon chopped fresh rosemary
Olive oil, for drizzling	1 teaspoon chopped fresh chives
	1 teaspoon chopped fresh parsley
	Kosher salt and freshly ground black pepper

Clean the mushrooms and cut off any tough parts from the stems. If using large chanterelles, halve or quarter them; if using cremini, halve or quarter them, depending on size. Finely mince the shallots. Cut the tomatoes into small chunks.

Preheat the broiler. Toast the bread until golden brown. Cut the garlic clove in half and rub it back and forth across the craggy surface of the pieces of bread. Place each piece on a serving plate and drizzle with olive oil.

Roast the poblano over medium-high heat on the stovetop or under the broiler, turning occasionally, until blackened and blistered all over. Place the chile in a bowl, cover with plastic wrap, and let it steam for 10 minutes.

Meanwhile, bring a large pot of lightly salted water to a boil over high heat. Holding a spear of asparagus by its tip and its tail, bring the ends together; the bottom will snap off at the point where its bitterness ends. Trim the rest of the asparagus to approximately the same length. Add the asparagus to the boiling water and cook for 3 minutes; it will still be crisp. Drain and let cool.

Pat the asparagus dry and dice it.

Peel the poblano with your fingers (do not rinse) and seed it. Dice it and toss it with the minced shallots.

Melt 2 tablespoons of the butter in a large skillet over medium heat. Add the mushrooms and cook until tender, about 5 minutes. Add the shallots and chile, reduce the heat to low, and cook, stirring occasionally, for 5 minutes, until softened. Add the Madeira, stirring to release any browned bits on the bottom of the pan, and bring to a simmer. Reduce the heat and simmer gently for 10 minutes, stirring occasionally.

Add the asparagus, tomatoes, and herbs. Season with salt and pepper, add the remaining 4 tablespoons butter, and cook, stirring, until the butter is melted and the vegetables are heated through.

Top each toast with some of the mushroom ragout and serve warm.

TUNA CARPACCIO

4 servings

Tuna, with its intrinsic beefy texture and almost meaty flavor, is a good candidate for the carpaccio treatment. You need extremely fresh tuna with great color. Cucumber adds a crunchy contrast and the confetti effect of the peppers creates visual excitement. In winter, jicama makes a good substitute for the cucumber. Hothouse cucumbers have little to say for themselves and should be avoided if possible.

You can slice and pound the tuna a few hours ahead of time. (Freezing it for an hour makes it easier to slice.) Be careful not to pound the tuna too hard, and be sure to pound in the direction of the grain.

¾ pound sushi-quality tuna, preferably bluefin

Mayonnaise
1 lime
½ cup extra-virgin olive oil
2 large egg yolks
2 tablespoons champagne vinegar or rice wine vinegar
2 tablespoons whole-grain mustard

Kosher salt and freshly ground black pepper
1 cucumber
1 tablespoon diced red bell pepper
1 tablespoon diced yellow bell pepper
1 tablespoon diced green bell pepper
1 tablespoon chopped fresh chives
1 organic marigold flower, for garnish (optional)

Place the well-wrapped tuna in the freezer for an hour to facilitate slicing.

Slice the tuna against the grain into 4 equal pieces. Cut four 12-inch squares of parchment paper. Lightly oil the paper. Place a slice of tuna on one half of a piece of paper, fold the paper in half over the tuna, and pound it lightly with a kitchen mallet or a rolling pin to about a 6-inch square. Repeat with the remaining tuna slices. (The tuna can be refrigerated, still covered with the paper, on a plate for up to 2 hours.)

MAKE THE MAYONNAISE
Juice the lime. Pour the olive oil into a measuring cup or pitcher with a narrow spout. In a medium bowl, whisk together the egg yolks, vinegar, mustard, and lime juice for 2 minutes. Whisking, slowly dribble in a few teaspoons of olive oil until the sauce begins to emulsify. Still whisking, slowly drizzle in the rest of the olive oil in a thin stream—not too fast, or the mayonnaise will "break," or curdle. If the mayonnaise is stiff, thin it with a little hot

water; it should be light and fluffy. Season with salt and pepper.

Peel the cucumber. Halve it lengthwise, remove the seeds, and cut it into fine julienne. Toss the strips with ¼ cup of the mayonnaise.

Place the cucumber strips on a platter. Place the tuna on top of the cucumber. Place a dab of mayonnaise on top of each slice, or use a squirt bottle to make a pretty zigzag pattern. Mix the diced peppers together and sprinkle the plates with them, then sprinkle with the chives. Garnish with marigold petals, if you have them. Serve.

SEAFOOD CEVICHE

4 servings

Ice-cold, extremely fresh seafood bursting with the tangy flavors of chilled citrus juices and crunchy bits of pepper and onion is a nearly perfect midsummer dinner appetizer or afternoon snack. During hot, humid July nights in New York City in the 1990s, ceviche became the most popular starter in town.

Ceviche doesn't have a set formula governing its ingredients. You need only to find impeccably fresh seafood and go from there. The multileveled flavors and different acidities of grapefruit, oranges, and/or tangerines in combination with the traditional lemons and limes make for a more complex ceviche. The only rules are not to marinate the fish any longer than specified, or it will turn to mush and taste more like marinade than fish, and to keep all the utensils, serving bowls, fruits, vegetables, and fish as cold as possible.

This goes well with a simple garden salad. Wine is not my first choice for serving with ceviche; a cold beer or a tropical cocktail is better.

1	orange	¼	garlic clove
1	tangerine	¼	pound bay scallops
1	grapefruit	¼	pound medium (25–30 per pound) shrimp
1	lime	¼	pound salmon or halibut fillet
1	lemon	¼	cup fresh cilantro leaves
1	red bell pepper	¼	cup extra-virgin olive oil
1	yellow bell pepper		Kosher salt and freshly ground black pepper
1	jalapeño chile	1	small bunch fresh chives
1	small red onion		

Slice the tops and bottoms off the orange, tangerine, and grapefruit with a sharp paring knife, exposing the fruit. Stand each fruit on a cutting board and, following the contours of the fruit, slice off the peel in strips from top to bottom, making sure to remove the bitter white pith. To remove the segments, hold each fruit in the palm of your hand and, working over a medium bowl, gently slice along each membrane to release the whole segments, letting them drop into the bowl. Juice the lime and lemon and add the juice to the citrus sections.

Core, seed, and dice the bell peppers. Stem, seed, and finely dice the jalapeño. Cut the red onion crosswise in half and finely mince. Mince the garlic.

Remove the tough muscle from the side of each scallop. Peel and devein the shrimp. Coarsely chop the shrimp and scallops. Cut the salmon or halibut into small cubes.

Add the bell peppers, jalapeño, onion, garlic, cilantro, olive oil, and a little salt and pepper to the bowl with the citrus. Stir in the scallops, shrimp, and fish. Cover and let marinate in the refrigerator for 1 hour.

When ready to serve, mince the chives. Remove the ceviche from the marinade with a slotted spoon and place on four plates. Garnish with the chives and serve.

DEEP-FRIED SQUID WITH CHIPOTLE MAYONNAISE

4 to 6 servings

Most of the squid available in the United States has been frozen, but the flavor and texture of fresh squid are completely different. If fresh squid is available, it's messier to deal with, but it's worth the trouble. If you don't live near a seaport, though, fresh is probably out of the question.

Fried squid goes beautifully with a ramekin of chipotle mayonnaise for dipping. Chipotle chiles—smoked jalapeños—are most often sold canned in a spicy adobo sauce. They are becoming more and more widely available all the time and can be found in many supermarkets, as well as through Internet sources.

To fry the squid, you'll need a deep-fryer or a large heavy pot. You'll also need a wire frying basket that fits in the pot or a "spider" or Chinese mesh skimmer (or a slotted spoon).

The trick is maintaining the oil at the proper temperature. The difference between good frying and bad also depends on timing and using the right oil, one with a high smoking point, but most important is the temperature.

Be prepared when you fry. Be sober, alert, and clothed appropriately. If you've got a splatter screen, by all means use it. Splatters are always a hazard. Enough sermonizing: follow along, you'll be fine.

2 pounds squid or 12 ounces
    cleaned squid
2 cups milk

Mayonnaise
1 cup olive oil
2 tablespoons pureed canned chipotle
    chiles with adobo sauce
3 large egg yolks

2 tablespoons fresh lemon juice
    Kosher salt and freshly ground black
    pepper

½ bunch fresh parsley
1 lime
2 cups corn oil or peanut oil
2 cups fine cornmeal
½ cup minced red bell pepper
½ cup minced green bell pepper

IF NECESSARY, CLEAN THE SQUID

Gently pull the body of each squid away from the head. Slice off the tentacles in one piece and discard the head. Remove the hard "beak" found in the center of the tentacles. Pull out the plasticlike quill and the viscera from each body. You can leave on the fine purple skin or pull it off. Rinse out the bodies and rinse the tentacles. (If using cleaned squid, simply rinse it well.)

With a sharp knife, cut the bodies into ¾-inch-wide rings. Leave the tentacles whole. Place the squid in a bowl, cover with the milk, and refrigerate for at least 1 hour.

MAKE THE MAYONNAISE

Pour the olive oil into a measuring cup or pitcher with a narrow spout. Place the puree in a medium bowl. Whisk in the egg yolks and lemon juice, then whisk for 2 minutes. Whisking, dribble in a few teaspoons of the olive oil until the sauce begins to emulsify. Still whisking, drizzle in the rest of the olive oil in a thin stream—not too fast, or the mayonnaise will "break," or curdle. You may need to whisk in a little hot water to adjust the consistency; the mayonnaise should be light and fluffy. Season with salt and pepper. Cover and refrigerate.

Wash the parsley, pull off the stems, and pat the leaves thoroughly dry. Wrap in a paper towel, put in a plastic bag, and refrigerate until ready to use. Slice the lime and set aside.

Heat the corn or peanut oil in a deep-fryer or large pot to 370 degrees. Put the cornmeal in a brown paper bag. Drain the squid and shake off the excess liquid. Toss it into the bag with the cornmeal. To fry the squid all at once, place the squid in a wire basket and shake off the excess cornmeal. Carefully add the squid to the hot oil. With the wire basket, push the squid down to the bottom of the pot to ensure proper crisping. If you have a splatter screen, set it over the pot. When the squid is golden brown, 4 to 6 minutes, remove and drain on paper towels.

Alternatively, fry the squid in batches, removing it with a spider or mesh skimmer, or a slotted spoon. Keep warm. Be sure to allow the oil to return to the proper temperature between batches.

Carefully add the parsley to the hot oil—be very careful of splattering—and fry for 30 seconds to 1 minute, or until lightly browned. Drain on paper towels.

Divide the squid among four to six plates or put it all on a platter. Set out the chipotle mayonnaise in small ramekins or in one larger one if you're serving the squid on a platter. Garnish the squid with the lime slices, sprinkle on the fried parsley, and finish with a scattering of the minced peppers. Serve immediately.

FRIED SHRIMP WITH CAPER MAYONNAISE

6 servings

I've eaten shrimp from the sea in Taiwan, from the bay in North Carolina, Maine shrimp from the rivers, Santa Barbara shrimp from the Pacific, and Hawaiian shrimp from a kind of plastic saltwater pond. My favorite? Maine shrimp.

Almost all the shrimp in the market has been frozen, but don't be put off by the idea of frozen shrimp. Shrimp does freeze well. If you happen to live near a coastal shrimp village, though, consider yourself lucky.

Mayonnaise
1 lemon
2 large egg yolks
1 tablespoon Dijon mustard
1 tablespoon red wine vinegar
1 tablespoon capers, drained
1 tablespoon chopped fresh parsley
¼ teaspoon red pepper flakes
1 cup olive oil
  Kosher salt and freshly ground
    black pepper

3 cups corn oil or peanut oil
2 cups all-purpose flour
1 teaspoon kosher salt
1 cup dry white wine
2 pounds large (16–20 per pound) shrimp,
    peeled and deveined
  Sea salt

MAKE THE MAYONNAISE
Juice the lemon. In a medium bowl, whisk together the yolks, mustard, vinegar, capers, parsley, and pepper flakes, then whisk for 3 minutes. Pour the olive oil into a measuring cup or pitcher with a narrow spout. Whisking, dribble in a few teaspoons of olive oil until the sauce begins to emulsify. Still whisking, slowly drizzle in the rest of the olive oil in a very thin stream—not too fast, or the mayonnaise will "break," or curdle. Season with as much lemon juice as you like. If the mayo is too thick, thin it with a little hot water; it should be light and fluffy. Season with salt and pepper.

Heat the oil in a wide pot or deep heavy skillet over medium-high heat to 350 degrees. Meanwhile, combine the flour, kosher salt, wine, and 1 cup water in a shallow bowl and mix thoroughly to make a smooth batter.

Working in batches, coat the shrimp in the batter, letting the excess drain off. Add to the hot oil and fry until crispy and golden brown, 2 to 3 minutes; do not crowd. Remove with a slotted spoon and drain on paper towels, then sprinkle with sea salt. Serve with the mayonnaise.

HOT OYSTERS WITH BLACK PEPPER BUTTER

This recipe is so easy you'll suspect there must be a hitch—there isn't. Hog Island oysters from Tomales Bay and Fanny Bays from Puget Sound are particularly wonderful—briny and firm with a fruity finish—but use whichever oysters are best in your area.

You'll need a grill grid—a wire cooling rack will suffice.

Kosher salt or rock salt
  for stabilizing the oysters
2 oysters per person

1 tablespoon unsalted butter per person
½ teaspoon cracked black peppercorns
  per person

Prepare a medium-hot fire in a grill. Spread a ½-inch layer of salt on a serving platter.

Clean the oysters, scrubbing them with a stiff brush, and rinse well.

Melt the butter in a small saucepan and cook until golden brown. Stir in the pepper. Keep warm.

Lay a grid over the grill's cooking grate. Place the oysters on the grid and cook them just until they pop open.

Pull off the top shells and nestle the oysters on the bed of salt. Spoon a generous teaspoon of the black pepper butter onto each hot oyster and serve immediately.

BEEF CARPACCIO
WITH WARM POTATO SALAD

6 first-course or lunch servings

Carpaccio was a famous Renaissance painter, but in modern times, we are more inclined to associate the term with thin sheets of raw meat. Supposedly, the dish—simplicity itself—was invented at Harry's Bar in Venice. It's a bit shameless, but it's undeniably delectable. I've reconstructed the original dish into a more substantial and even more luxurious one, using filet mignon, the crown jewel of the meat world. The combination of potatoes and lettuce is wonderful with the delicious cold beef.

Serve it as a main course at lunch or as an appetizer at dinner. Note that the dressing should stand for at least 1 hour for the flavors to develop.

Vinaigrette

- 2 tablespoons sherry vinegar
- 1 teaspoon kosher salt
- 3 tablespoons walnut oil
- ¼ cup olive oil
- 2 shallots

- ¾ pound trimmed filet mignon

Mayonnaise

- ½ cup olive oil
- 2 large egg yolks
- 2 tablespoons fresh lemon juice
  Kosher salt and freshly ground
      black pepper

- 4 Yellow Finn potatoes
  or small white potatoes
- 1 lime
- 1 head red leaf lettuce
- 2 tablespoons minced fresh chives
  Fresh parsley sprigs, for garnish

MAKE THE VINAIGRETTE

Whisk the sherry vinegar and salt in a medium bowl. Slowly whisk in the walnut oil, then whisk in the olive oil. Mince the shallots and add them to the vinaigrette. Let it stand at room temperature for at least 1 hour.

PREPARE THE CARPACCIO AND POTATOES

Cut the beef across the grain into 6 equal pieces. Cut twelve 12-inch-square pieces of parchment paper. Oil each of the parchment sheets on one side. Place one sheet of parchment on a hard work surface. Place one piece of beef on the oiled sheet of parchment, lay a second piece of parchment, oil side down, over the meat, and, with a heavy mallet, pound it to a rough 8-inch circle. Patch any tears by pushing the meat back together, and set aside. Repeat with the remaining 5 pieces. Stack the carpaccio, still sandwiched between the parchment, and refrigerate.

MAKE THE MAYONNAISE

Pour the olive oil into a pitcher or a measuring cup with a narrow spout. Whisk the egg yolks with the lemon juice in a medium bowl, then whisk for 3 minutes. Whisking, dribble in a few teaspoons of oil until the sauce begins to emulsify. Still whisking, drizzle in the rest of the oil in a very thin stream—not too fast, or the mayonnaise will "break," or curdle. Dribble in ¼ cup hot water, whisking. Season lightly with salt and pepper.

Peel the potatoes and cut them into ¼-inch-thick rounds. Place in a saucepan of cold water and bring to a boil, then reduce the heat and simmer for 10 minutes, or until just tender. Drain.

Add the potatoes to the mayonnaise and mix well.

Cut the lime into wedges; set aside. Separate the lettuce leaves, wash, and dry. Toss the lettuce with 2 tablespoons of the vinaigrette. Decorate the plates with the lettuce leaves, rib sides down, starting in the center with the smaller leaves, and arrange the larger leaves around the perimeter. Spoon the potato salad onto the center of the plates.

Remove the carpaccio from the refrigerator. One at a time, slowly peel back the top sheet of parchment paper, invert the slice of meat onto the lettuce and potatoes, pressing down slightly to push the meat slightly into the potatoes, and carefully peel off the remaining sheet of parchment. Dress the carpaccio lightly with the remaining vinaigrette. Garnish with the minced chives, parsley sprigs, and lime wedges.

ROASTED ONION, SEARED STEAK, AND ONION RINGS

4 servings

For this unusual dish, roasted onions are stuffed with thin slices of barely seared filet mignon, which is topped with a mixture of crème fraîche, chopped roasted onion, and toasted cumin. The result can then be scattered with hot beer-battered onion rings. (The onion rings are optional.)

I originally created the onion rings for my friend the late Bruce Paltrow, one of Hollywood's best TV drama producers, when I was the chef at Michael's in Santa Monica. The Paltrows were exuberant eaters, and Bruce in particular knew a lot about food. He often complained that I didn't serve onion rings. One evening, to surprise him, I concocted a batter based on his favorite beer (Heineken), and sliced some incredibly sweet Maui onions, and fried them up. The onion rings never made it onto the menu, but whenever Bruce or one of his cronies came around, we would whip up a batch, serving them furtively to hide them from nearby diners.

4 large firm red or white onions,
  unpeeled
Olive oil
Kosher salt and freshly ground
  black pepper

Fried onion rings (optional)
1 cup all-purpose flour
½ teaspoon kosher salt
1 cup lager
2 large eggs, separated
1 large red or white onion
2 cups milk
2 cups corn oil or peanut oil
Sea salt

8 ounces filet mignon
Olive oil
½ cup crème fraîche
1 teaspoon cumin seeds
Watercress sprigs, for garnish (optional)

Heat the oven to 400 degrees.

ROAST THE ONIONS

Coat the unpeeled onions with a little olive oil and salt and pepper them. Place them on a small baking sheet and roast for 1 hour, or until the skins are black and the onions are tender when pierced with a skewer. Remove from the oven and let cool.

MEANWHILE, START THE OPTIONAL FRIED ONION RINGS

Whisk the flour and salt in a medium bowl. Stir in the beer and egg yolks. Set the batter aside until you're ready to deep-fry.

Slice the onion into ¼-inch-thick rings. Place the rings in a bowl, cover with the milk, and set aside.

POUND THE BEEF

Slice the filet mignon against the grain into 4 portions. One at a time, coat each piece of meat with olive oil, place it between 2 sheets of plastic wrap, and pound it gently with a clean mallet or rolling pin until it's ⅛ inch thick and twice the original size. Place the meat on a plate, cover, and refrigerate until you're ready to cook it.

STUFF THE ONIONS

Peel the roasted onions. Pop out the center (approximately half) of each onion and finely chop the centers. Combine the chopped onion with the crème fraîche in a medium bowl.

In a small dry skillet, toast the cumin seeds over medium heat just until fragrant, about 3 minutes. Pulverize the seeds with a mortar and pestle or in an electric spice grinder and add the cumin to the crème fraîche mixture.

SEAR THE BEEF

Heat a large dry cast-iron or other heavy skillet over medium-high heat for 5 minutes. Quickly sear the beef, in batches if necessary, on one side only. Set aside.

Place a roasted onion shell on each of four plates. Roll up the slices of beef and nestle them in the onion shells. Spoon about 2 tablespoons of the crème fraîche mixture onto the beef, dividing it equally.

FRY THE OPTIONAL ONION RINGS

Heat the oil in a deep pot to 375 degrees. Meanwhile, beat the egg whites in a medium bowl to soft peaks with an electric mixer. Fold the whites into the beer batter. Working in batches, remove the onion rings from the milk, coat them in the batter, and deep-fry until golden, turning once, 3 to 4 minutes. Remove with a slotted spoon and drain on paper towels. Salt the onion rings judiciously with sea salt.

Scatter the onion rings over the stuffed onions, garnish with the watercress if desired, and serve.

CRISPY CHICKEN AND GOAT CHEESE BURRITOS

12 burritos, serving 6

This is a variation on one of the most popular appetizers I served at my first restaurant, Jams, in New York City. They are incredibly addictive: people frequently ordered them as a first course and then turned around and had another serving as a main course, and no matter how many we made, we'd always run out of them on Saturday nights.

These aren't really burritos. I don't know precisely what qualifies a burrito as a burrito, but the tortillas are corn rather than flour, and there aren't any beans involved here. The truth is they really are more like flautas or crispy tacos, but I liked the term "burrito," and it has stuck.

The filling is delicious even without its tortilla shell—it's fantastic on pasta or spread on toasts, like rillettes or pâté.

4	large chicken legs	1	lemon
2	tablespoons chili powder	1	lime
	Kosher salt and freshly ground black pepper	1	bunch scallions
		6	tablespoons (¾ stick) unsalted butter
1	red bell pepper	8	ounces soft fresh goat cheese
1	green bell pepper	1	cup fresh cilantro leaves
2	jalapeño chiles	12	6-inch corn tortillas
2	medium onions		Guacamole (page 19), for garnish (optional)
10	garlic cloves		
¼	cup olive oil		

Heat the oven to 400 degrees.

Sprinkle the chicken legs with the chili powder and salt and pepper and place in a roasting pan. Roast the legs for 30 minutes, or until the meat is cooked through and the skin is crispy. Allow to cool. Remove the chicken skin and meat from the bones; shred the meat and thinly slice the skin. Place the skin and meat in a bowl.

Roast the bell peppers and chiles over medium-high heat on the stovetop or under a hot broiler, turning occasionally, until blackened and blistered all over. Place them in a bowl, cover with plastic wrap, and let them steam for 15 minutes.

Peel the peppers and chiles with your fingers (do not rinse) and stem and seed them. Chop the peppers and chiles and add them to the chicken, along with any liquid that has collected in the bowl.

Mince the onions and garlic. Heat the olive oil in a large skillet over medium heat. Add the onions and garlic and cook, stirring occasionally, until the onions are very tender, about 15 minutes.

Meanwhile, juice the lemon and lime (separately) and set the juices aside. Finely chop the scallions. Melt the butter and set aside in a warm spot.

Add the peppers, chiles, and chicken to the onion mixture and stir well, then add ½ cup water and bring to a simmer.

When the water in the skillet is almost evaporated, turn off the heat, add the lemon juice, and mash well with a large fork. Transfer to a bowl, add the goat cheese, and mix well. Add the minced scallions, cilantro, and lime juice. Taste for seasoning and add salt and pepper if needed.

Heat the oven to 400 degrees.

To assemble the burritos, lay a tortilla on a flat surface and place ¼ cup of the chicken mixture in the center. Carefully fold over the two sides and press slightly, then fold over the top and bottom of the tortilla and press again to form a neat package. Brush a baking sheet with the melted butter. Place the burritos seam side down 1 inch apart on the baking sheet, Bake, turning once, for 20 minutes, until each side is crispy.

Arrange on serving plates or a platter and garnish with the guacamole if desired.

SOUPS

**THE TRUE TEST
OF ANY COOK IS
HIS OR HER ABILITY TO
MAKE A SIMPLE SOUP.**

The true test of any cook is his or her ability to make a simple soup. Producing a magnificent lobster soup or an elegant wild mushroom soup requires patience and a bit of skill, but the techniques themselves are delightfully few. I've selected some diverse offerings that will convince you that homemade soups really can be an everyday affair. You're sure to find that once you've mastered a few soups and chowders, any store-bought version will pale in comparison.

The most interesting and tantalizing soups are often those made with only two or three vegetables, a bit of chicken stock, and a handful of herbs and seasonings that are cooked together slowly. The richest and most flavorful of all vegetable soups are based on rich, meaty vegetables, like eggplant. Soups made from these vegetables can be as satisfying and hearty as any meat-based ones, without their heaviness.

The fish soups in this chapter rely on forceful fish stocks flavored with aromatic vegetables, which are then married with a variety of good fresh fish or shellfish. The more intense the flavor of your base stock, the better the final soup.

Garnishes are too often an afterthought. With a simple vegetable soup, a swirl of pesto or perhaps a dollop of flavored cream will add a final, all-important flavoring component. In elaborate fish chowders and stews, a puree of smoked salmon makes all the difference. Instead of just serving a loaf of bread, treat your guests to soup topped with lusty garlic croutons or cheese-encrusted thin slices of rye, or, on black bean soup, a scattering of freshly fried thin tortilla strips.

SOUPS

Always remember that your ingredients' intrinsic flavors will be by necessity diluted in a soup. An aging onion or a mediocre tomato will become completely insipid. Start with the best—tomatoes bursting with flavor but too full of juice to use in a salad, sweet and tangy onions—and your soup will sing out loud.

CHILLED EGGPLANT AND ROASTED PEPPER SOUP

8 first-course servings

Eggplant and peppers combine in this spicy, peppery cool soup that serves well as an opening foray but is substantial enough for a main course. You'll find that these two ingredients are at their peak flavor in the latter part of summer, but, due in part to a good supply of South American eggplants and Dutch bell peppers, the soup can be made the whole year around. Make sure your eggplant is firm to the touch, with bright, shiny skin.

The soup can be made well in advance. You can even press it into service as a dip, if you like, by using less liquid when pureeing the soup.

2 large eggplants
½ cup olive oil
   Kosher salt and freshly ground
      black pepper
4 red bell peppers
2 large white onions
   (about 5 ounces each)
2 garlic cloves
4 tablespoons (½ stick) unsalted butter
2 cups chicken broth or water
2 bay leaves
3 fresh tarragon sprigs

Ginger cream
2 tablespoons minced peeled fresh ginger
½ cup heavy cream
   Kosher salt and freshly ground black
      pepper
1 tablespoon chopped fresh thyme

   Thyme blossoms, for garnish (optional)

Heat the oven to 400 degrees.

Cut the eggplants lengthwise in half. Score the flesh lightly, toss them in 2 tablespoons of the olive oil, and season lightly with salt and pepper. Place cut side up on a baking sheet and roast until soft, 20 to 30 minutes. Set aside to cool.

Roast the peppers over medium-high heat on the stovetop or under a hot broiler, turning occasionally, until blackened and blistered all over. Place them in a bowl, cover with plastic wrap, and let them steam for 15 minutes.

Working over the bowl, peel the peppers with your fingers (do not rinse); reserve the juices that collect in the bottom of the bowl. Stem and seed the peppers and cut them into 1-inch squares. Return the pepper pieces to the bowl and toss them with 2 tablespoons of the olive oil.

Halve the onions and slice them crosswise as thin as possible. Mince the garlic.

Heat the butter in a large heavy saucepan over medium heat. Add the onions and garlic and cook, stirring occasionally with a wooden spoon, until the onions are translucent, 5 to 10 minutes. Add the peppers and cook for 5 minutes, stirring occasionally.

Coarsely chop the eggplants. Heat the remaining ¼ cup olive oil in a large cast-iron casserole or Dutch oven over high heat. Add the eggplant, season with salt and pepper, and cook, stirring occasionally, until golden brown, about 8 minutes. Deglaze the pan with the chicken broth or water. Stir well, add the onion mixture, and bring to a simmer. Add the bay leaves and tarragon, reduce the heat, and simmer gently for 30 minutes. As the soup cooks, you can add a little water if necessary, but keep it on the thick side.

Remove the bay leaves and tarragon sprigs and taste the soup for seasoning. It should be slightly salty. Let cool.

Puree the soup with an immersion blender or in batches in a regular blender, adding a little water if it seems too thick. Pour into a bowl, cover, and refrigerate until cold.

MAKE THE GINGER CREAM

Place the ginger in a small saucepan, add 1 cup water, and bring to a simmer. Cook gently for 10 minutes, until the ginger is tender. Drain the ginger in a sieve, reserving the liquid, and set aside in a medium bowl.

Return the cooking liquid to the saucepan and boil until reduced to 2 tablespoons. Add to the bowl with the ginger and let cool.

Add the cream to the ginger and beat with an electric mixer until the cream holds soft peaks. Season with a little salt and pepper and the thyme.

Serve the soup cold or at cool room temperature—it shouldn't be too cold, or the flavors will be muted. Ladle into soup bowls, float a dollop of ginger cream on top, and decorate with thyme blossoms, if you've got them.

CORN SOUP WITH SAFFRON
8 first-course servings

This is one of my most favorite soups. Using corncobs for the base rather than a chicken stock not only makes the soup vegetarian but gives it a remarkably pure flavor.

The season for corn appears to be endless now that the harvest starts in South America and travels northward. The new hybrid varieties stay sweet long after they've been picked. When you're making corn soup, remember to taste the corn raw to check the relative sweetness, and, if necessary, add more cream to dilute the soup a bit.

8 ears corn
1 dried red chile
1 small bunch fresh parsley
4 garlic cloves
1 large sweet onion, such as Vidalia
4 tablespoons (½ stick) unsalted butter

¼ cup chopped fresh cilantro
 Pinch of saffron threads
½ cup heavy cream
 Kosher salt and freshly ground
  black pepper
 About ¼ cup chopped fresh chives, for
  garnish

Husk the corn and slice off the kernels with a sharp knife (reserve the cobs). Transfer the corn to a bowl, cover, and refrigerate.

Place the cobs in a large saucepan, add 2 quarts water, the chile, parsley, and garlic, and bring to a boil. Lower the heat and simmer for 2 hours. Strain the stock and set aside.

Thinly slice the onion. Melt 3 tablespoons of the butter in a medium saucepan over medium-low heat. Add half of the corn kernels and the onion and cook, stirring occasionally, for 10 to 15 minutes, or until the onion is tender.

Reserve ½ cup of the corn stock and pour the rest into the saucepan with the corn and onion.

Add the cilantro and bring to a boil, then lower the heat and simmer for 45 minutes. Remove from the heat.

Meanwhile, in a small skillet, combine the reserved ½ cup corn stock and the saffron threads, bring to a simmer, and simmer until the stock is highly flavored, 5 to 10 minutes. Remove from the heat and let cool.

Puree the soup with an immersion blender or in batches in a regular blender. Strain it into a clean saucepan.

Beat the cream in a medium bowl with an electric mixer until it holds soft peaks. On low speed, drizzle in the saffron stock. Cover and refrigerate until ready to use.

Place the remaining corn kernels and the remaining 1 tablespoon butter in a large skillet and cook over medium-low heat, covered, for 10 minutes. Season with salt and pepper.

Add the corn to the pureed soup and bring to a simmer. Taste and season with salt and pepper if necessary.

Serve the soup in warm bowls, topped with a dollop of saffron cream and a scattering of snipped chives.

VIDALIA ONION AND SWEET CORN SOUP

6 to 8 first-course servings

Vidalia onions are the pride of Georgia, along with the state's famous peaches, quail, and magnolias. These onions first appear around the end of April or beginning of May. That season is short, ending in June, but they are now grown in the fall as well, giving consumers a second chance at them. Equally wonderful sweet onions are grown in other parts of the country. All sweet onions have a limited shelf life. They should be firm and exude a milky white juice when they're sliced.

If you'd like to add a little minced serrano chile to balance the sweetness of the soup, go for it.

4 sweet onions, such as Vidalia	4 cups chicken broth
4 tablespoons (½ stick) unsalted butter	2 teaspoons chopped fresh flat-leaf parsley
2 tablespoons olive oil	½ teaspoon chopped fresh tarragon
Kosher salt and freshly ground black pepper	½ cup heavy cream (optional)
4 ears white corn	1 small serrano chile (optional)

Slice the onions. Heat the butter and oil in a large heavy saucepan over medium heat. Add the onions, season with salt and pepper, and cook, stirring occasionally, for 15 to 20 minutes, or until soft and golden.

Meanwhile, husk the corn and slice off the kernels with a sharp knife.

Add the corn to the onions and cook for 10 minutes, or until cooked through. Add the chicken broth, bring to a boil, reduce the heat to low, and simmer for 20 to 30 minutes.

Stir the parsley and tarragon into the soup. Add the cream, if using, and heat through. Taste for salt and pepper. If you like, finely mince the serrano chile and stir some or all of it in. Serve hot.

BUTTERNUT SQUASH AND JONATHAN APPLE SOUP

4 first-course servings

My great-uncle grew Jonathan and Gravenstein apples on his hilltop farm near Co-tati, California. When I was growing up in the San Francisco Bay Area, my parents would take my brothers and me up there to spend the weekends. At the end of those long Indian summers, the fragrance of the fallen apples fermenting on the ground was intoxicating.

The Jonathan is one of the best cooking apples. I wanted to combine its crisp perkiness with the deep nutty flavor of butternut squash. The apple cider binds this vegetarian soup with tart staying power.

1 **medium butternut squash** (about 2 pounds)	1 **medium white onion**
7 **tablespoons unsalted butter,** at room temperature	2 **garlic cloves**
	Freshly ground black pepper
Kosher salt	2 **cups fresh apple cider**
3 **Jonathan, McIntosh,** or Jonagold apples	

Heat the oven to 350 degrees.

Cut the squash lengthwise in half and scoop out the seeds. Place the squash cut side up in a small roasting pan, dot with 3 tablespoons of the butter, and season with salt. Roast for 1 hour.

Meanwhile, cut the apples in half and remove the stems, cores, and seeds. Add the apples to the roasting pan and roast for 30 minutes, or until the squash and apples are tender. Let the squash cool slightly, then scoop out the flesh and coarsely chop it. Coarsely chop the apples.

Slice the onion into thin rounds. Peel and smash the garlic.

Melt the remaining 4 tablespoons butter in a large saucepan over medium heat. Add the onion and garlic, season with salt and pepper, and sauté, stirring occasionally, for 15 minutes, or until tender. Add the squash and apples. Pour in the cider and 2 cups water and bring the soup to a boil, then reduce the heat to low and simmer for 20 minutes.

Puree the soup with an immersion blender or in batches in a regular blender, adding water to thin it if necessary. Taste and season with salt and pepper to taste. Rewarm the soup if necessary and serve.

WILD MUSHROOM AND LEEK SOUP

6 to 8 first-course servings

The chewy stems and gnarly bits from the mushrooms and the dark green tops of the leeks make a rich, flavorful stock that serves as the base for this forcefully flavored vegetarian soup.

1½ pounds mixed mushrooms, such as shiitakes, portobellos, chanterelles, morels, and hedgehogs
1½ pounds leeks
8 garlic cloves
1 medium onion
6 tablespoons olive oil

1 fresh thyme sprig
2 bay leaves
  Kosher salt and freshly ground black pepper
¼ cup chopped fresh flat-leaf parsley
2 cups dry white wine
  Garlic Croutons (page 78)

Clean and trim the mushrooms, keeping the stems and caps separate. Wash the leeks thoroughly. Thinly slice the leeks, keeping the dark green tops separate. Finely mince the garlic and onion.

Heat 3 tablespoons of the olive oil in a large saucepan over low heat. Add the mushroom stems, the dark green portions of the leeks, half the garlic, the onion, thyme, bay leaves, and salt and pepper to taste and cook for 5 minutes, stirring occasionally. Add the parsley, wine, and 2 quarts water. Increase the heat to medium and bring to a simmer, then reduce the heat and simmer gently, skimming the foam that rises to the surface, for 1 hour.

Strain the stock into a clean saucepan and keep warm.

Cut the mushroom caps into ½-inch dice. In a large enameled cast-iron casserole or Dutch oven, heat the remaining 3 tablespoons olive oil over medium heat. Add the whites of the leeks, the remaining garlic, and the mushrooms. Season lightly with salt and pepper and cook for 10 minutes, or until tender. Add 6 cups of the stock, bring to a boil, reduce the heat to low, and simmer for 30 minutes. Taste for seasoning. Serve with the garlic croutons.

BLACK BEAN SOUP

8 servings

Dense, meaty black beans require very little preparation other than checking them carefully to remove any stones and soaking them for about 8 hours before cooking. To make this recipe vegetarian, leave out the ham hock. Even without it, the soup will have an appealing smokiness from the chipotle chiles.

2	cups dried black beans
2	red onions
1	jalapeño chile
1	head garlic
2	tablespoons olive oil
1	ham hock
2	bay leaves
1	tablespoon minced canned chipotle chiles in adobo or good spicy store-bought salsa

½	cup fresh cilantro leaves (reserve the stems)
	Freshly ground black pepper
	Kosher salt
1	lime
1	cup crème fraîche or sour cream
¼	cup chopped fresh chives

Rinse and pick over the beans. Place in a bowl, add cool water to cover generously, and soak for at least 8 hours, or overnight. Drain.

Mince the onions; set aside ½ cup for garnish. Mince the jalapeño chile. Separate the head of garlic into cloves and peel them; leave the cloves whole.

Heat the olive oil in a large heavy saucepan over medium heat. Add the onions, garlic, and ham hock and cook, stirring occasionally, until the onions are light golden in color and the ham hock is browned, about 20 minutes. Stir in the beans, bay leaves, jalapeño, chipotle, cilantro stems, and a teaspoon of black pepper (don't

add salt—it will toughen the beans' skins). Add 2 quarts cold water and bring to a boil, then reduce the heat to low and simmer for 1 to 2 hours, or until the beans are very tender.

Remove the soup from the heat and fish out the ham hock and bay leaves. Take the meat off the bone and dice it. Discard the ham bone and the bay leaves. Season the soup with salt and more pepper if needed and add the ham meat. Reheat the soup until hot. Halve the lime.

To serve, ladle the soup into bowls and top each with a dollop of crème fraîche. Sprinkle with the reserved minced onion, chives, and chopped cilantro. Finish with a squeeze of lime juice.

MUSSEL AND LITTLENECK CLAM CHOWDER
6 to 8 servings

The beauty of this soup lies in its many colors and creamy texture. I've always found chowders delicious, yet somehow they usually play basically the same tune. Here I've spiced things up by adding coconut, orange zest, zucchini, and saffron. These ingredients lend an exotic yet harmonious note.

3	small onions	3	new potatoes or other small potatoes
3	garlic cloves	3	small carrots
2	serrano chiles	2	small zucchini
1	2-inch piece fresh ginger	4	tomatoes
¼	cup unsweetened shredded coconut	½	cup fresh cilantro leaves
1	pint littleneck clams	4	fresh sage leaves
1	pint mussels	1	lime
2	tablespoons olive oil	1½	cups heavy cream
2	cups dry white wine		Kosher salt and freshly ground
	Grated zest of 1 orange		black pepper
1	teaspoon saffron threads		

Heat the oven to 300 degrees.

Thinly slice the onions. Mince the garlic. Stem and mince the chiles. Peel the ginger and cut it into tiny strips.

Spread the coconut on a baking sheet and toast in the oven for 5 minutes, or until lightly colored, stirring once. Transfer to a plate.

Meanwhile, clean the clams and mussels, scrubbing them with a stiff brush, and rinse well. Discard any with cracked or gaping shells. Remove the beards from the mussels. Place the clams and mussels in separate bowls and refrigerate until ready to use.

Heat the olive oil in a large pot over low heat. Add the onions, garlic, and chiles, cover, and cook for 5 to 8 minutes, or until the onions are softened. Add the wine, orange zest, ginger, and ½ teaspoon of the saffron and cook for 10 minutes. Increase the heat to medium and bring the mixture to a boil, then add the clams to the pot. Add the mussels after 1 minute and cook just until the clams and mussels start to open. Turn off the heat and, with a slotted spoon, remove the mussels and clams as they open. Remove all the meat from the shells and place in a bowl; cover and refrigerate. Discard the shells. Strain the cooking liquid through a fine-mesh strainer into a large clean saucepan; set aside.

Peel and slice the potatoes. Peel and dice the carrots. Dice the zucchini. Halve and chop the tomatoes. Chop the cilantro and sage. Juice the lime.

Bring the cooking liquid to a boil. Add the potatoes, carrots, zucchini, and tomatoes, reduce the heat and simmer until all the vegetables are tender. Add the cream, coconut, and herbs. Add the remaining ½ teaspoon saffron and the mussels and clams and heat through. The chowder will be soupier than a traditional chowder.

Season the soup with salt and pepper and stir in lime juice to taste. Ladle the soup into bowls and serve hot.

COD AND CALAMARI STEW
6 to 8 servings

This is a variation on traditional Mediterranean seafood stew. The fish broth is infused with the heady flavor of orange zest, which stands up well to the cod and bolsters the delicate squid.

Fresh squid is essential here, so if you can't find it, either leave it out or try another recipe.

2 pounds fish bones from nonoily white-fish, including heads if possible	¼ teaspoon red pepper flakes
1 pound squid or ½ pound cleaned squid	¼ teaspoon coriander seeds
2 garlic cloves	¼ teaspoon black peppercorns
1 red onion	1 cup dry white wine
1 medium bunch fresh cilantro	1 large tomato
1 orange	1 pound cod fillet
3 tablespoons olive oil	Kosher salt and freshly ground black pepper

Rinse the fish bones. Remove any gills and discolored flesh from the heads, if using, and rinse thoroughly. With kitchen shears, cut the bones into smaller pieces (quarter the heads). If necessary, clean the squid (see page 39).

Smash the garlic and finely mince it. Chop the onion. Remove the cilantro leaves from the stems, and reserve the stems. Zest and juice the orange.

Place the garlic and 1 tablespoon of the olive oil in a large pot and sauté the garlic gently, stirring, over medium-low heat, until softened. Stir in the onion and cook gently, stirring, until softened. Stir in the red pepper flakes, coriander seeds, and black peppercorns, then add the

white wine, orange zest and juice, and cilantro stems. Add all the fish bones and pour in enough water to cover, about 4 cups. Bring just to a boil, then immediately reduce to a simmer and cook for 45 to 50 minutes. Strain the broth.

Meanwhile, dice the tomato. Cut the cod into small cubes. Rinse the squid thoroughly and cut the bodies into rings. Slice the tentacles into smaller pieces if they are large.

Heat the remaining 2 tablespoons olive oil in an enameled cast-iron casserole or Dutch oven over medium-low heat. Toss in the cod and squid, then add the strained broth, cilantro leaves, and tomato and heat to a simmer. Simmer gently just until the cod is cooked through. Season with salt and pepper to taste and serve.

LOBSTER AND TOMATO BISQUE
4 to 6 first-course servings

Here is a certain crowd-pleaser. I've often thought that lobster bisques were a bit heavy and tomato soups a bit thin—this maximizes the two in one bowl. The richness of the lobster is delicately offset by the slightly acidic tomatoes. The techniques are straightforward, and the two soups can be easily made in advance and reheated, or not—the soup can also be served cold. When I wonder what to serve guests at an important dinner, I realize that this is it.

1	1½-pound live lobster
1	large red onion
6	garlic cloves
¼	cup olive oil
4	red tomatoes
1	cup dry white wine
1	cup heavy cream

1	onion
4	yellow tomatoes
2	yellow bell peppers
	Kosher salt and freshly ground black pepper

In a large pot, bring 2 cups water to a boil. Add the lobster, cover, and cook for 10 minutes.

Remove the lobster from the pot and let cool, then extract its meat; reserve the shells and the cooking liquid. Dice the lobster meat, cover, and refrigerate.

Mince the red onion and garlic.

MAKE THE RED TOMATO SOUP
Break up the lobster shells and place them in a large heavy saucepan with 2 tablespoons of the olive oil. Add the minced red onion and half the garlic and sauté over medium heat for 5 minutes.

Dice the red tomatoes. Add the wine, lobster cooking liquid, and red tomatoes to the saucepan, bring to a simmer, and cook for 45 minutes. Strain the soup into a clean saucepan if serving hot or into a bowl if serving cold. Add the diced lobster meat and the cream.

MEANWHILE, MAKE THE YELLOW TOMATO SOUP
Mince the onion. Heat the remaining 2 tablespoons oil in a medium saucepan over medium heat. Add the onion and the remaining garlic and sauté for 5 minutes.

Dice the yellow tomatoes and yellow peppers and add them to the pan. Reduce the heat and simmer for 45 minutes. Strain the soup into a clean saucepan or a bowl.

Season each soup with salt and pepper.

If serving hot, gently reheat each soup. If serving cold, cover each soup and refrigerate until chilled.

To serve, divide the yellow soup among four to six bowls, then swirl in the red tomato soup in a decorative pattern. Serve hot or cold.

IT USED TO BOTHER
ME WHEN PEOPLE AT
DINNER PARTIES
ASKED ME TO
DRESS THEIR SALADS.
WHY WOULD ANYBODY
WANT ANOTHER COOK
MESSING UP THE WORKS?

SALADS

The dish that put me off greens was Caesar salad. My mother, armed with the authentic recipe she'd gotten from Caesar himself in the early 1960s, tried to enlist my help in making it. The romaine lettuce wasn't the problem, nor was it the garlic croutons, the olive oil, or the lemon. But when she approached me with those raw egg yolks—that was it! I fled the scene. Only one salad did whet my appetite: a wedge of iceberg with blue cheese dressing.

During my rock-and-roll years, I finally began to eat greens. And by greens I mean watercress, dandelion and mustard greens, herbs, beet and turnip tops, all types of cabbage, and any combo of exotic Asian or European greens. Ironically, it was the fabulous Caesar salad at Vanessi's, *the* San Francisco restaurant of the 1960s and 1970s, that finally lured me in. From then on, I couldn't live without salad. Now I'm a Caesar salad expert. The coddled egg, the crisp green romaine spears, and the croutons send me into ecstasy.

I've planted gardens so I could have greens straight from the field. I've paid exorbitant amounts of cash to farmers to get them to grow specific types of greens. An important revelation during my years in France was the warm salad: a mixture of soft and bitter greens tossed with a warm vinaigrette, causing the greens to wilt slightly, sometimes topped with warm cooked vegetables.

Use bright green, fruity, light olive oils for salads. The country of origin is not as important as the manufacturer, and the type of processing. For salads, use only oils that are cold-pressed and from the first pressing; this is noted on the bottle as extra-virgin. Please try as many oils as you can get your hands on, remembering that olive oil is perishable and can go rancid quickly. A good bit of advice is to buy only ½-liter bottles, no larger—these will be more expensive than bigger containers, but you'll always have fresh oil.

I love salt on a plain green salad. Vinegar or acid completes the taste for me.

SALADS

GARDEN SALAD

4 servings

There is inspiration in compliments. It used to bother me when people at dinner parties asked me to dress their salads. Why in the world would anybody want another cook messing up the works? Finally, when one friend told me his dressings always tasted greasy and flat, I started to analyze what made mine different. What was that inexplicable detail that could make all the difference? First, have good ingredients (that seems obvious), and second, always add the vinegar first. "That can't be all there is to it," my friend said. He was right—there is a more difficult matter: how much dressing to use.

Here is my formula.

About 8 cups loosely packed
    wonderful greens (radicchio,
    mizuna, arugula, oak leaf, butter,
    romaine, spinach, endive, trevise,
    frisée, tatsoi, dandelion)

Freshly ground black pepper
Balsamic vinegar
Green, fruity extra-virgin olive oil

Wash and dry the lettuces and put them in a salad bowl. Add black pepper to taste—a little salt—to the greens and toss well. Add a smidgen of vinegar and toss again, then look the greens over carefully and see if they look slightly moistened. If you're satisfied, add a few teaspoons of olive oil, no more, and toss well. If the salad glistens, you've added enough oil, but taste it after tossing two more times, to make sure. That's it.

TWO THREE-TOMATO SALADS

It's hard for me to cook a ripe summer tomato. The longer it cooks, the more the fruit's natural acidity overcomes its sweetness. A voluptuously ripe tomato picked at its peak in late August is perfect as it is. The most you might do to enhance it would be to slice up a few of these tomatoes and toss them in a simple vinaigrette, using the best olive oil and just a little vinegar, as in this recipe.

This title is a slight misnomer. The name of the salad should really be Multiple-Tomato Salad. The number of types of tomatoes that could be used to make either version of the salad may be as high as one hundred. And that's not even as many as those cultivated by some people I know, namely the Chinos in Rancho Santa Fe, California, and Elizabeth Berry in Chaco Canyon, New Mexico, who at last count was growing more than 125 different types of tomatoes. Today the markets are full of tiny currant tomatoes, large multicolored Marvel Stripe tomatoes, dark-green-and-yellow-splotched grape tomatoes with emerald-green juice, and dozens of others.

Three-Tomato Salad, Version 1

4 servings

About 1 pound tomatoes, in varying sizes and varieties, from tiny to medium
¼ cup extra-virgin olive oil
1 tablespoon good red wine vinegar
Sea salt and freshly ground black pepper
Fresh purple or green basil leaves or chervil sprigs

Slice the larger tomatoes and arrange them, alternating colors, on four plates. Leave currant tomatoes whole and slice cherry tomatoes in half. Slice the remaining tomatoes into quarters or eighths, and arrange on the plates. Scatter the currant or cherry tomatoes over them.

Whisk the olive oil and vinegar in a small bowl.

Sprinkle the salads with salt and pepper to taste. Spoon on a little of the vinaigrette at the last possible moment. Decorate with basil leaves or chervil. Serve at room temperature, never chilled.

Three-Tomato Salad, Version 2

8 servings

2   pounds mixed large ripe red, yellow,
      green, orange, and/or striped
      tomatoes
1   pound small to tiny assorted
      tomatoes
¼   cup loosely packed fresh red
      or purple basil leaves, plus
      a few leaves for garnish
¼   cup loosely packed fresh green
      basil leaves, plus a few leaves
      for garnish

1   tablespoon good red
      or white wine vinegar
      Sea salt and freshly ground
      black pepper
¼   cup extra-virgin olive oil,
      or more to taste

Slice the large tomatoes ⅛ inch thick and alternate them in overlapping circles on eight plates.

Leave the small tomatoes whole or cut them in half. Set aside.

Stack the basil leaves, a handful at a time, roll them into a cigar, and slice into very fine julienne strips. Place the basil strips in a small bowl and add the vinegar and salt and pepper to taste. Whisk in the oil and taste for seasoning.

Dribble some of the vinaigrette over the plated tomatoes. Toss the small tomatoes in the remaining vinaigrette and scatter them over the plates. Garnish with a little more pepper and the basil leaves. Serve at room temperature, never cold.

SESAME-CRUSTED GOAT CHEESE CAKES ON GREENS

8 first-course servings

These black-and-white-sesame-seed-coated cakes of goat cheese are both dramatic and delicious. You'll need quite a lot of white and black sesame seeds. Shops in Chinatown or Indian markets often sell sesame seeds in bulk for a lot less than you'd pay for two or three spice bottles at your supermarket—where you probably won't find the black seeds anyway. You can also buy them online at www.penzeys.com. (If you don't get black or brown sesame seeds, just double the amount of white seeds—the visual effect won't be as striking, but the dish will still be very good.)

This dish can be served as a warm appetizer salad or at room temperature as a red-wine-friendly savory after a meat or poultry entrée. The sesame oil lends an Asian note, and the sherry vinegar cuts the richness of the goat cheese nicely.

½ cup white sesame seeds

½ cup black or brown sesame seeds
    (see headnote)

    Kosher salt and freshly ground
    black pepper

2 tablespoons unsalted butter

8 shallots, not peeled

1 tablespoon olive oil

¼ cup sherry vinegar

2 tablespoons toasted sesame oil

¼ cup plus 1 tablespoon extra-virgin
    olive oil

1 8-ounce log soft fresh goat cheese,
    at room temperature

½ cup fresh basil leaves

4 cups loosely packed mesclun
    Nasturtiums, for garnish (optional)

Heat the oven to 325 degrees.

Spread the white and black sesame seeds on separate baking sheets and lightly toast in the oven, 8 to 12 minutes, stirring once. Sprinkle them with salt and pepper, pour onto two separate plates, and let cool. Leave the oven on.

Meanwhile, melt the butter. Cut a 12-inch square of parchment, fold it in half, and unfold it. Place the unpeeled shallots on one half of the paper and drizzle with the melted butter and the 1 tablespoon olive oil, tossing to coat. Salt and pepper the shallots, fold the other side of the piece of paper over them, and fold over the edges of the parchment all around, making a double fold to seal them.

Place the package on a baking sheet and roast for 30 to 40 minutes, or until the shallots are just tender. Remove the packet from the oven and let cool.

Unfold the parchment and pour the shallot cooking oil into a small bowl. Peel the shallots, leaving them whole.

Place the sherry vinegar in a medium bowl. Whisking constantly, slowly dribble in the sesame oil, then slowly add the ¼ cup extra-virgin olive oil and the shallot oil. Stir in the shallots. Season with salt and pepper to taste.

Heat the oven to 325 degrees again. Brush a baking sheet with the remaining 1 tablespoon oil.

Cut the goat cheese into 8 equal "cakes." Put the white sesame seeds in a small deep bowl and put the black seeds in a second bowl. Dip and roll half of each cake in the white sesame seeds, then roll the other half in the black seeds, to create a two-toned effect. Place on the baking sheet and bake for 5 to 8 minutes, or until the cheese is just warm but not melting.

Shred the basil leaves and toss with the lettuce in a medium bowl. Toss again with just enough of the vinaigrette to coat the greens lightly. Arrange on salad plates and top with the goat cheese cakes. Serve warm or at room temperature, garnished with nasturtiums, if you like.

WILD MUSHROOM SALAD

8 first-course servings

I concocted this recipe while I was chef at Michael's in Santa Monica. I wanted a warm wilted salad that still had crunch and the complexity to stand alone. The method of simply dumping a hot item—bacon and bacon fat, for example—on top of greens resulted in the right texture, but not the right intensity of flavors. I decided instead to add the vinaigrette to the mushrooms in the pan, heating it enough to wilt the lettuces, so they would harmoniously take on the flavor of both mushrooms and vinaigrette. The salad became so popular that I had to take it off the menu occasionally because of varying mushroom availability: wild mushrooms are seasonal. We produce domesticated shiitakes, oyster mushrooms, and other types in this country, and they will do, but don't expect the flavor to be the same as the wild versions.

Garlic croutons

- 2 cups 1-inch cubes sourdough bread
- 2 garlic cloves
- 2 teaspoons chopped fresh rosemary
- 2 tablespoons olive oil

- ¼ cup pine nuts
  Kosher salt
- 1 pound mixed wild mushrooms, such as chanterelles, morels, shiitake, hedgehog, and cèpes (porcini)
- ¼ pound thinly sliced prosciutto or good smoked ham

- 1 shallot
- ¼ cup sherry vinegar
- 2 tablespoons hazelnut oil
- 2 tablespoons walnut oil
- ¼ cup chopped fresh chives
- 4 fresh sage leaves, chopped
  Freshly ground black pepper
- 5–6 cups mixed torn firm lettuces, such as endive, radicchio, and romaine
- ½ cup loosely packed red, purple, or green basil leaves
- 2 tablespoons olive oil

MAKE THE GARLIC CROUTONS
Heat the oven to 350 degrees.

Place the bread cubes on a baking sheet and bake until golden, 8 to 10 minutes. Meanwhile, mince the garlic.

Put the croutons in a medium bowl and sprinkle with the rosemary and olive oil. (Leave the oven on.) Add the garlic and toss.

Put the pine nuts in a pie pan or on a small baking sheet and toast in the oven for 3 to 5 minutes, or until just golden. Don't overcook—

they burn easily! Pour into a bowl and season with salt to taste.

Meanwhile, clean the mushrooms by cutting away any rough spots and brushing away any dirt. Slice the mushrooms into bite-sized pieces, toss together in a bowl, and set aside.

Slice the prosciutto into thin 1-inch-long strips. Set aside.

Mince the shallot and place it in a small bowl. Add the vinegar, then dribble in the hazelnut and walnut oils, whisking constantly. Stir in the chives, sage, and pepper to taste.

Put the lettuces in a large salad bowl, add the basil, and toss well.

Heat the olive oil in a large skillet over medium-high heat until almost smoking. Add the mushrooms, season with salt and pepper, and toss well. Cook, stirring occasionally, until the mushrooms are turning golden. Quickly add the vinaigrette, stir well, and remove from the heat. Immediately add the mixture to the lettuces and toss once. Add the pine nuts, prosciutto, and croutons and toss vigorously. Taste for seasoning, adding salt and pepper if needed, and divide among eight plates. Serve quickly, before the lettuce can become soggy.

GREENS, PANCETTA, AND POACHED EGG SALAD

4 first-course servings or 2 main-course servings

Faced with the quandary of coming up with a special egg dish at my restaurant Bud's in New York City, I recalled an extraordinary meal I'd had in the Beaujolais region of France at a two-star restaurant, the Auberge du Cèpe in Fleurie. I had gone there to research the possibility of purchasing a vineyard property and villa, neither of which, unfortunately, lived up to my expectations. The meal, however, more than compensated. The highlight was a salad called "la Beaujolaise." It was a mix of greens, bacon, and an egg poached in Beaujolais. I thought the salad, with a little interpolation, might be well suited for lunch on the Upper West Side.

¼ pound thinly sliced pancetta
½ pound shiitake mushrooms
    Freshly ground black pepper
2 cups dry red wine, preferably
    Beaujolais
¼ cup red wine vinegar

1 bunch curly endive (chicory)
1 tablespoon whole-grain mustard
¼ cup extra-virgin olive oil
4 extremely fresh large eggs

Cut the pancetta into thin strips and sauté in a large skillet over low heat until fairly crisp. Using a slotted spoon, remove the pancetta and drain it on paper towels, leaving the fat in the pan.

Meanwhile, clean the mushrooms, remove and discard the stems, and slice the caps into bite-sized pieces. Add the mushrooms to the skillet, pepper them lightly, and sauté over medium heat until lightly browned.

While the mushrooms cook, pour the red wine and 2 tablespoons of the vinegar into a medium saucepan and bring to a simmer over low heat.

Wash and dry the endive and place it in a large bowl.

Add the pancetta and the mushrooms, with the hot pancetta fat, to the endive and toss well.

Deglaze the mushroom pan with the remaining 2 tablespoons vinegar. Stir in the mustard, then whisk in the oil. Cook for 1 to 2 minutes.

Meanwhile, poach the eggs in the simmering wine mixture until just set, 1 to 2 minutes. Remove them with a slotted spoon and drain on paper towels.

Season the vinaigrette carefully with pepper, then vigorously toss the salad with the vinaigrette. Divide the salad among serving plates and top each with 1 or 2 warm poached eggs. Serve promptly.

WARM DANDELION, BACON, AND POTATO SALAD

4 first-course servings or 2 main-course servings

A true bacon salad needs to be warm and crunchy, which means it must be assembled at the last possible moment. Dandelion is an inexpensive leaf that marries well with bacon. The sage adds a wonderfully stimulating flavor to the proceedings. Warming the dandelion leaves three times, tossing them first with the roasted potatoes, then with the hot bacon and fat, and finally with the sautéed shallots, wilts them nicely and softens any bitterness.

2 tablespoons unsalted butter	3 medium shallots
4–6 new potatoes or other small potatoes	4 fresh sage leaves
2 garlic cloves	4 chive blossoms, for garnish (optional)
Kosher salt and freshly ground black pepper	¼ cup plus 2 tablespoons olive oil
¼ pound thick-cut bacon	1 tablespoon whole-grain mustard
1 bunch dandelion greens, 10–12 inches long, or mustard greens	¼ cup sherry vinegar

Heat the oven to 400 degrees.

Melt the butter; keep warm. Cut the potatoes into ¼-inch-thick slices. Smash and peel the garlic. Spread the potatoes in a roasting pan in a single layer and add the garlic. Salt and pepper the potatoes and drizzle them with the butter. Roast the potatoes for 20 to 30 minutes, or until golden and tender.

While the potatoes are roasting, cut the bacon crosswise into ½-inch-wide pieces to make "lardons." Set aside.

Wash the greens. Cut off the bitter bottom stalks. Cut the leaves into 3-inch lengths and place them in a bowl. Mince the shallots. Finely chop the sage leaves. Separate the chive blossoms, if using, into individual florets.

When the potatoes are done, discard the garlic and toss the warm potatoes with the greens.

Place the bacon and the 2 tablespoons olive oil in a large skillet and cook over medium heat, stirring occasionally, until the bacon is just golden brown. Using a slotted spoon, add the hot bacon to the dandelion leaves. Pour in 2 tablespoons of the rendered bacon fat and toss well.

Add the shallots to the remaining bacon fat and sauté them briefly, just until softened. Remove them with the slotted spoon and add them to the dandelion mixture.

Carefully add the mustard and sherry vinegar to the pan, whisking well, then add the sage. Turn the heat down to low and add the remaining ¼ cup olive oil, whisking until the dressing has emulsified. Immediately pour it over the greens. Toss well and season with ¼ teaspoon black pepper.

Divide the salad among serving plates and garnish with the chive blossoms, if using. Serve immediately.

WARM SQUID SALAD

4 first-course servings or 2 main-course servings

I conceived this salad in 1991 at Table 29 restaurant in Napa, California, and it received such a great response that it became a menu standby. It's a variation on a warm wilted salad, but this time it's the heat of the rapidly seared squid that melts the greens. The hot squid is enrobed with sweet red pepper aïoli and tossed with toasty bread crumbs: it's a wonderful combination of soft, crispy, and spicy. The freshness of the squid is the only hitch—frozen will not suffice. However, you could quite readily substitute other seafood, cut into bite-sized pieces, such as shrimp, fresh lobster meat, or halibut.

1 cup soft fresh bread crumbs
½ pound mixed crisp greens, such as mizuna, frisée, endive, and escarole
2 pounds squid or 12 ounces cleaned squid
1 garlic clove
2 tablespoons olive oil, or as needed

Kosher salt and freshly ground black pepper
½ cup light fish stock or dry white wine
2 tablespoons champagne vinegar or rice wine vinegar
2 tablespoons extra-virgin olive oil
1 cup Aïoli (page 102)

Heat the oven to 300 degrees.

Spread the bread crumbs on a baking sheet and lightly toast in the oven, about 8 minutes.

Meanwhile, wash and dry the lettuces. Tear into 2-inch pieces and place in a large bowl.

If necessary, clean the squid (see page 39).

Cut the squid into 1-inch lengths and dry well. Mash the garlic and finely mince it.

Heat a large skillet over high heat. Add the oil and heat until it almost smokes. Salt and pepper the squid and carefully slide it into the skillet in batches; do not crowd. The squid will stick to the bottom of the pan at first; as soon as it "releases," quickly turn the pieces over. Transfer the cooked squid to a medium bowl and cover to keep warm; add more oil to the pan as necessary for the remaining batches. When all the squid is cooked, turn the heat down to low, add the garlic to the pan, and cook, stirring, until lightly browned. Scrape the garlic into the bowl with the squid. Cover to keep warm.

Deglaze the skillet with the fish stock or white wine, then bring to a simmer and let reduce for a few minutes. Whisk in the vinegar and then the extra-virgin olive oil, whisking until the mixture is emulsified. Remove from the heat, add the red pepper aïoli, and whisk well, then pour the sauce over the squid.

Add half of the bread crumbs to the squid mixture and toss twice, then add the squid to the greens and toss well. Divide the salad among serving plates, sprinkle with the remaining bread crumbs, and serve immediately.

LOBSTER AND POTATO CHIP SALAD

6 first-course servings or 4 main-course servings

In this spectacular, colorful salad, roasted red peppers, lobster, and lettuce are beautifully set off by green beans and crispy golden potato chips. Alice Waters taught me how to make this vinaigrette at Chez Panisse many years ago. Her style is evident in many of the dishes I do, both consciously and subconsciously. If it weren't for Alice, I think I would have been just another struggling, easily frustrated cook. Perhaps the most important thing I learned from her was not recipes, but a simple yet tough and uncompromising message: it is a professional basic that you must taste everything you buy and make. Whatever you serve must meet your standards, and only then is the food fit for public consumption. This notion may seem obvious, but it is the most difficult concept to get across to new cooks, possibly because we are such a visually oriented society, and food is no exception. If it looks good, they reason, it must be good. Alice always railed against such an idea: taste is of ultimate importance. Bobby Flay puts it another way: "If you're not chewing, you're not cooking."

2	1½-pound lobsters	1	pound green beans
1	russet potato	1	head oak leaf lettuce
¾	cup extra-virgin olive oil	¼	cup balsamic vinegar
	Kosher salt and freshly ground	¼	cup loosely packed purple
	black pepper		or green basil leaves
2	red bell peppers		

Heat the oven to 400 degrees.

Bring a large pot of salted water to a boil. Add the lobsters and cook for 8 to 10 minutes, or until you see a white substance (collagen) at the widest part of the tail. Pull the lobsters out of the water and drain on a platter. When they're cool enough to handle, remove the meat from the shells and slice into bite-sized chunks. Refrigerate.

Peel the potato and slice as thin as possible or use a mandoline. Place in a bowl, add ¼ cup of the olive oil, and season with salt and pepper, turning the slices carefully to coat. Spread the potatoes out on two baking sheets in a single layer and bake, turning once, until crispy and golden brown, 20 to 30 minutes. Remove from the oven and drain on paper towels.

Roast the peppers over medium-high heat on the stovetop or under a hot broiler, turning occasionally, until blackened and blistered all over. Place the peppers in a bowl, cover with plastic wrap, and let them steam for 15 minutes.

Meanwhile, bring a large saucepan of water to a boil. Top and tail the beans. Generously salt the boiling water, add the beans, and cook for 5 minutes, or until crisp-tender. Drain and spread them on paper towels to cool.

Wash the lettuce and pat dry.

Peel the peppers with your fingers (do not rinse) and stem and seed them. Slice them into ½-inch-wide strips; save any juices in the bowl for the vinaigrette.

Whisk together the remaining ½ cup extra-virgin olive oil and the balsamic vinegar in a small bowl. Add any pepper juices and season with salt and pepper.

In a large bowl, toss the lettuce with the basil. Add the beans and lobster and toss gently. Toss again with the vinaigrette, and arrange the salad on a platter. Decorate it with the potato chips and pepper strips and serve.

SWEETBREAD AND CELERY ROOT SALAD

4 first-course servings or 2 main-course servings

This unusual salad is just right for cold autumn or winter nights. But don't hesitate if you get the craving for sweetbreads in the spring.

Most cooks are apprehensive when they confront sweetbreads (thymus and pancreas glands of a young calf) for the first time. But if you follow the instructions in this recipe, you will discover that they're surprisingly easy to prepare and that they're also quite beautiful once cooked. You will need to blanch the sweetbreads in the court bouillon the day before you serve the salad. Two notes of caution: Always use sweetbreads as soon as possible after purchasing them—they don't keep well. And under- or overcooking sweetbreads renders them inedible.

1 pound white, firm, plump fresh or frozen sweetbreads (defrosted if frozen)
1 medium white onion
4 garlic cloves
1 jalapeño chile
¼ cup white wine vinegar
1 bouquet garni (see page 5)
  Kosher salt
1 tablespoon black peppercorns

1 pound celery root
½ cup heavy cream
4 tablespoons (½ stick) unsalted butter
  Freshly ground black pepper
¼ pound thick-cut bacon
¼ cup olive oil
1 head savoy cabbage
¼ cup champagne vinegar or rice wine vinegar
  Fresh flat-leaf parsley leaves, for garnish

Soak the sweetbreads in cold salted water for 2 hours, changing the water once or twice, to get rid of any blood. Drain.

MEANWHILE, MAKE A COURT BOUILLON

Thinly slice the onion and garlic. Cut the jalapeño in half. Place the onion, garlic, and jalapeño in a medium saucepan and add the white wine vinegar, 4 cups water, the bouquet garni, 1 teaspoon salt, and the peppercorns. Bring to a simmer and simmer for 30 minutes.

Add the sweetbreads to the court bouillon and simmer until just cooked through (firm, not hard, to the touch), about 12 minutes. Remove the sweetbreads to a colander with a slotted spoon and run under cold water to stop the cooking. Pour the court bouillon into a bowl and let cool, then add the sweetbreads, cover, and refrigerate overnight.

The next day, drain the sweetbreads and discard the liquid. Peel the membranes off the sweetbreads using your fingers and remove noticeable fat and any extraneous material. Slice the sweetbreads into ½-inch-thick rounds. Cover and refrigerate.

Peel the celery root with a sharp knife and cut it into 1-inch cubes. Place the cubes in a small saucepan, cover with cold water, add 1 tablespoon salt, and bring to a simmer. Cook until just tender, 25 to 30 minutes.

Drain the celery root, transfer it to a food processor, and add the cream and 2 tablespoons of the butter. Process to a puree, then return to the saucepan and add salt and pepper to taste. Set aside.

Slice the bacon into ¼-inch-wide strips. Place them in a large skillet with 2 tablespoons of the olive oil and cook over medium heat until browned. Turn off the heat. Using a slotted spoon, transfer the bacon to paper towels to drain, leaving all the fat in the pan.

Tear off the tough outer leaves of the cabbage and discard them. Separate the remaining leaves and slice them into ½-inch-wide strips. Heat the fat remaining in the skillet over medium-high heat. Add the cabbage and stir until wilted, about 3 minutes. Add the champagne vinegar and simmer until the cabbage is tender, 8 to 10 minutes. Season with salt and pepper, turn off the heat, and cover to keep warm.

Heat the remaining 2 tablespoons butter and 2 tablespoons oil in a large skillet over medium-high heat. Salt and pepper the sweetbreads, add to the pan, in batches if necessary, and sauté until nicely browned on each side, 3 to 4 minutes per side; don't crowd the pan. Remove the sweetbreads to a platter and cover to keep them warm.

Meanwhile, reheat the celery root puree.

Spoon a little of the puree into the center of each of two or four warm plates. Top with the sautéed sweetbread slices, surround with the cabbage, and sprinkle with the bacon strips. Decorate the plates with parsley leaves.

SMOKED SALMON, QUAIL EGGS, AND ENDIVE

4 first-course servings or 2 main-course servings

The combination of poached quail eggs, smoked salmon, and potatoes is widely appreciated by the British. In England, the potatoes are often roasted in the fireplace (standard in households there), but here they're oven-roasted. The smoked salmon should be from a good source. Quail eggs are available in Chinese markets and some specialty shops, as well as online from D'Artagnan (online at www.dartagnan.com or 800-327-8246).

2	pounds new potatoes or other small potatoes
4–6	tablespoons (½–¾ stick) unsalted butter, as needed
	Kosher salt and freshly ground black pepper
1	lemon
2	tablespoons champagne vinegar or rice wine vinegar
¼	cup olive oil
3	Belgian endives
1	pound sliced smoked salmon
12	quail eggs
1	teaspoon cracked black peppercorns
	Minced fresh dill

Heat the oven to 400 degrees.

Wash the potatoes and cut them into wedges. Place 2 tablespoons of the butter in an ovenproof skillet large enough to hold the potatoes in a single layer, or use two skillets and double the butter. Heat the butter over medium-high heat until bubbling, then put the potatoes cut side down in the hot butter. Salt and pepper the potatoes, transfer the skillet(s) to the oven, and roast for 20 minutes, or until the potatoes are just tender.

Meanwhile, make the vinaigrette: Juice the lemon. Combine the lemon juice and vinegar in a medium bowl. Slowly add the olive oil, whisking until emulsified.

Slice off the root ends of the endives and separate into spears. Place the endive spears on serving plates, arranging them like the petals of a flower. Reserve 3 tablespoons of the vinaigrette and drizzle the rest over the spears. Divide the smoked salmon among the plates, draping it over the endive leaves.

When the potatoes are done, toss them in the reserved vinaigrette and arrange them around the salmon.

Melt the remaining 2 tablespoons butter in a large skillet over medium-high heat. To fry the quail eggs, slit each one open by making a small puncture in the pointed end of the egg with a small sharp pair of scissors and snipping down the side of the shell to release the yolk and white intact into the pan. Fry just until the yolks are set. With a small spatula, place 3 or 6 fried quail eggs on top of each serving of salmon. Sprinkle the plates with the cracked peppercorns and dill and serve at once.

I LIKE
CRUNCH
(IN THE BREAD),
SPICE
(IN THE SAUCE),
AND CRISPNESS
(IN THE FILLING).

SANDWICHES AND PIZZA

I was a notoriously fussy eater as a child, so I didn't learn to appreciate the finer world of sandwiches until I was much older. It was globe-trotting that made them such an important part of my life. The pivotal moment came at Harry's Bar in Venice. For customers like me who were crammed into the tiny bar space and whose tables were hours away from being ready, the bartender prepared a sort of peace offering: a tiny grilled ham and Fontina cheese sandwich. It was only about two inches wide, made of crustless hearty white bread and filled with lightly smoked pale ham and the nuttiest Fontina cheese. The diminutive sandwich had been fried in a copious amount of butter and was neatly wrapped in a parchment-paper triangle. It simultaneously satiated my appetite and whetted it for things to come.

The Harry's Bar sandwich had character. The sandwiches in this chapter are in that style. I like crunch (in the bread), spice (in the sauce), and crispness (in the filling). Sandwiches need good components: the best sliced meats, good thick-cut bacon, and condiments that are easy to make, unusual, and make the ingredients "pop."

Sandwiches can serve many masters. They can be as refined as the Avocado and Crab Sandwich. They can be glorious reincarnations of leftovers, like the Wilted Greens and Goat Cheese Sandwich, which puts two ingredients in perfect harmony, or Roast Chicken and Scallion Sandwich. The Smoked Salmon, Caviar, and Cream Cheese Sandwich can be an elegant hors d'oeuvre; the Shrimp BLT shines at brunch. And sometimes a sandwich can be the most satisfying meal in itself, needing nothing else but a cool glass of beer. The Pulled Beef and BBQ Sauce and Soft-Shell Crab and Aïoli Sandwiches being cases in point.

SANDWICHES AND PIZZA

Sandwiches have been made dramatically better in recent years by the resurgence of artisan bread makers and their magnificent loaves: whole-grain breads, crisp baguettes, Italian ciabatta. The array of recipes in this chapter reflects both my travels and my passion for what began long ago in English pubs as a thick slice of bread with cheddar cheese and in Italy as a soft slice of grilled focaccia with prosciutto. The sandwiches that follow aren't just lunchtime fare. Served with a salad, many make a spectacular dinner.

I've also included a family favorite, Pizza with Bacon, Scallions, Parmesan, and Tomato (my son loves bacon!), a wonderful addition to the sandwich family.

SMOKED SALMON, CAVIAR, AND CREAM CHEESE SANDWICH

4 to 6 servings

If I could, I would go to Fortnum & Mason in London every day for afternoon tea. I would start with champagne and salted, spiced nuts, followed by a sandwich like this one. I suggest using American hackleback or paddlefish caviar. Very close in taste and texture to traditional sevruga caviar, this caviar is from reliable suppliers and costs about one fourth the price.

Serve with a good bottle of champagne, preferably a rosé!

24	thin slices pain de mie (fine-grained white sandwich bread) or thin-sliced Pepperidge Farm bread
1	8-ounce package cream cheese, at room temperature
4	tablespoons (½ stick) unsalted butter, at room temperature

¼	cup crème fraîche
½	cup chopped fresh chives
2	ounces American hackleback or paddlefish caviar
½	pound thinly sliced Scottish or good domestic smoked wild salmon

Trim the crusts off the bread. Toast the bread very lightly. Let cool slightly.

Meanwhile, mix together the cream cheese, butter, crème fraîche, and chives.

Spread the cream cheese mixture evenly over the toast. Divide the caviar into 12 portions and gently spread it over 12 of the slices. Divide the smoked salmon into 12 portions and place it on the other 12 slices. Put the halves together, cut into halves or quarters, and serve on a platter.

WILTED GREENS AND GOAT CHEESE SANDWICH

4 sandwiches

Fresh goat cheese, minced sweet onion, and cooked greens make for a quick but sophisticated sandwich. At the restaurant, I use leftover greens from the dinner service; at home, I simply cook up whatever's in the fridge. You can use beet tops, spinach, romaine leaves, frisée, amaranth, or even herbs. The lightly spiced delicate cheese makes a perfect partner to the garlicky greens.

1 sweet onion, such as Vidalia	½ teaspoon red pepper flakes
3 garlic cloves	1 tablespoon chopped fresh
2 tablespoons olive oil	flat-leaf parsley
2 cups finely chopped greens	4 tablespoons (½ stick) unsalted butter,
(see headnote)	at room temperature
½ pound soft fresh goat cheese	8 slices sourdough bread
Kosher salt and freshly ground	
black pepper	

Slice the onion. Mince the garlic. Heat the olive oil in a large skillet over medium-high heat. Add the onion and cook, stirring occasionally, for 4 minutes, or until softened. Add the garlic and cook for about 1 minute, until softened.

Add the greens and if the greens are tough, up to ½ cup water. Cook the greens, stirring occasionally, until wilted and tender; tough greens may take as long as 10 minutes. Don't overcook. Drain the greens if necessary and let cool.

Meanwhile, mash the goat cheese with a fork in a medium bowl. Add salt and pepper to taste and the red pepper flakes.

Stir the greens and parsley into the goat cheese mixture and add salt and pepper to taste.

Lightly butter 4 slices of the bread. Spread the other 4 slices with the goat cheese–greens mixture and top with the buttered slices, buttered side up.

Melt about 1½ tablespoons of the remaining butter in a large skillet over medium-high heat (use two pans to speed up the process, if you like). When the butter begins to bubble, add one sandwich, unbuttered side down, and cook, turning once, until the bread is golden brown on both sides. Place the sandwich on a plate and cook the remaining sandwiches, adding more butter to the pan for each one.

Cut each sandwich into 4 wedges and serve.

AVOCADO AND CRAB SANDWICH

6 sandwiches

The filling for this sandwich is based on a traditional recipe for guacamole, but instead of the customary puree, the avocado is diced and then mixed with the other ingredients.

The choice of crabmeat is a delicate regional issue. I will state my preferences: First, lump crabmeat from Dungeness crab. No less spectacular, however, is Maine peekytoe crabmeat. And, of course, there is the ubiquitous blue crab from the Chesapeake and points south. This is the essence of a purist sandwich: "chopped" guacamole, crabmeat, and multigrain bread.

1 sweet onion, such as Vidalia	Kosher salt
1 cup fresh cilantro leaves	2 cups lump crabmeat
3 ripe Hass avocados	12 slices multigrain bread
1 Anaheim chile	2 garlic cloves, halved
2 limes	1 tablespoon olive oil

Mince the onion. Finely chop the cilantro. Halve, pit, peel, and finely dice the avocados. Stem, seed, and mince the chile. Juice the limes.

In a bowl, mix the onion, cilantro, chile, and lime juice. Add 1 teaspoon salt. Add the avocados. Lightly mash the ingredients together.

Pick over the crab to remove shells and cartilage. Season lightly with salt if necessary.

Toast the bread and rub each slice with the garlic. Sprinkle each slice of toast with olive oil. Spread the avocado mixture on half the slices of toast. Top with the crabmeat. Cover with the remaining toast slices.

Cut the sandwiches in half and serve.

SOFT-SHELL CRAB AND AÏOLI SANDWICH

4 sandwiches

I first had a taste of a crab po'boy in New Orleans in the early 1980s. It was beyond delicious—in the realm of food from heaven. The soft French roll, spicy mayo, and the gorgeous deep-fried crab, whose juices were literally dripping down my arm. What a sandwich!

My rendition calls for roasted crabs, as opposed to deep-fried. I marinate the crabs, then roast them, chop them, and toss them with aïoli. You'll find this version easier and less time-consuming, but the flavors are on an equal footing.

You can have the fishmonger clean the crabs, but in that case you should use them almost immediately. Or clean them yourself—I give instructions below.

4 soft-shell crabs, alive and kicking

Marinade

1   orange
2   garlic cloves
2   tablespoons olive oil
2   tablespoons dry white wine
1   teaspoon paprika

Aïoli

2   large egg yolks
3   garlic cloves
1   teaspoon kosher salt, or to taste
1   cup olive oil, or to taste

4   brioche buns or squares of focaccia, or the best buns you can find

Have your fishmonger clean the crabs or clean them yourself. Using scissors, cut away the eyes and mouth from each one. Fold back one side of the top shell, locate the gills, pull them away, and discard; repeat on the other side of the top shell. Turn the crab over. Fold back the tail flap, pull it away from the body, and discard. Put the crabs in a bowl.

MAKE THE MARINADE

Juice the orange. Mince the garlic. Whisk together the olive oil, white wine, orange juice, garlic, and paprika in a large bowl. Toss the crabs with the mixture, and refrigerate for 30 minutes or up to 2 hours.

Place the egg yolks in a blender. Add the garlic cloves and puree. Add the salt. On medium speed, dribble in a few teaspoons of olive oil until the sauce begins to emulsify. With the motor running, slowly drizzle in the rest of the oil—not too fast, or the mayonnaise will "break," or curdle. Add more salt if necessary. Transfer the aïoli to a large bowl.

Heat the oven to 400 degrees.

Remove the crabs from the marinade, without draining them thoroughly, and place on a rimmed baking sheet. Roast for 10 to 12 minutes, turning once, until golden brown and cooked through.

Chop each crab into 4 pieces and toss with the aïoli. Divide the crabs among the bottoms of the buns. Cover the sandwiches with the tops of the buns, cut them in half, and serve immediately.

SHRIMP BLT

6 sandwiches

My summers are family time. My father-in-law is from Wrightsville Beach, near Wilmington, North Carolina, and that sleepy, gorgeous stretch of sand is my wife's summer home.

Folks in North Carolina are great food lovers, especially when the local fishermen haul in the afternoon's shrimp catch. These gray-white beauties are sold flopping and alive. They are tremendous served right from the steamer, but they're equally fine in a sandwich.

Another prodigious product in this region is pork, and the bacon there is the best. The locals also grow some mighty delicious tomatoes. Throw all these together, and you have the makings of one damned good sandwich!

12 slices thick-cut bacon
2 pounds medium shrimp (26–30 per pound), preferably fresh, unpeeled
2 ripe, juicy tomatoes

Kosher salt
12 slices sourdough bread
1 cup mayonnaise (page 236)
6 leaves butter lettuce

Cook the bacon slowly in a large cast-iron skillet over medium-low heat. Remove the bacon and drain on paper towels.

Add the shrimp to the fat remaining in the skillet and cook over medium-high heat, turning once, until just cooked through, about 4 minutes. Remove the shrimp, let cool, and peel.

Slice the tomatoes and sprinkle with salt.

Lightly toast the bread. Spread mayonnaise on one side of each slice. Place a lettuce leaf, a tomato slice, and 2 slices of bacon on 6 slices of the toast. Top with the shrimp, dividing them equally, and then with the remaining toasts.

Cut diagonally in half and serve.

LOBSTER SALAD SANDWICH

6 sandwiches

My first experience with a lobster roll was transcendent. How could a hot dog bun slathered with butter and filled with just lobster meat and mayonnaise be *so* good?

I have adapted the classic to my tastes, with a fresh combo that's not as rich. I like the simplicity of the ingredients used here: a little olive oil, basil, succulent ripe tomatoes, fresh corn, and roasted bell pepper.

2 1-pound lobsters (culls, lobsters with only one claw, are fine)	2 red bell peppers
4 ears corn	15 fresh basil leaves
¼ cup olive oil	1 cup dry white wine
Kosher salt and freshly ground black pepper	3 ripe, juicy tomatoes
	1 regular baguette or 2 demibaguettes

Bring a large pot of salted water to a boil. Add the lobsters and cook for 10 minutes, or until you see a white substance (collagen) at the widest part of the tail. Pull the lobsters out of the pot and drain on a platter. When they're cool enough to handle, remove the meat from the lobsters. Cut the lobster meat into medium dice. Place in a medium bowl, cover, and refrigerate.

Husk the corn and cut the kernels from the cobs with a sharp knife.

Heat 2 tablespoons of the olive oil in a medium skillet. Add the corn and cook for about 2 minutes, or until just tender. Season to taste with salt and pepper. Remove from the heat and let cool.

Roast the peppers over medium-high heat on the stovetop or under a hot broiler, turning occasionally, until blackened and blistered all

over. Place the peppers in a bowl, cover with plastic wrap, and let steam for 15 minutes.

Meanwhile, in a blender, puree the basil with the wine and the remaining 2 tablespoons olive oil. Season to taste with salt and pepper.

Core and dice the tomatoes.

Peel the peppers with your fingers (do not rinse) and stem and seed them. Dice the peppers.

Add the tomatoes, corn, and peppers to the lobster and toss gently, then add the basil oil and toss again.

Heat the broiler. Split the baguette open and lightly toast it under the broiler. Top the bottom half (halves) with the lobster salad. Cover with the top(s) and cut into 6 equal lengths. Serve open-faced.

SPICY SWORDFISH SALAD SANDWICH

4 sandwiches

Here's a great opportunity to use up leftover swordfish or other mild fish. Try it with Spicy Swordfish (page 217) if you have any to spare. Serve with potato chips and pickles.

½ pound cooked swordfish or other leftover mild-flavored fish, cold from the refrigerator (about 10 ounces uncooked)

1 green bell pepper

1 cup Aïoli (page 102)

1 tablespoon capers, drained

1 tablespoon diced dill pickle

1 tablespoon chopped fresh chives

2 cups shredded iceberg lettuce

3 tablespoons extra-virgin olive oil
   Pinch of sea salt

1 ripe Hass avocado

8 slices country rye bread

Crumble the fish into flakes in a small bowl (you'll have 1½ to 2 cups).

Stem, seed, and dice the bell pepper. Combine with the aïoli, capers, pickle, and chives in a medium bowl. Add the fish and fold together well. Cover and refrigerate for at least 1 hour.

Toss the lettuce with the olive oil and salt. Halve, pit, peel, and slice the avocado.

Lightly toast the bread. Spread the swordfish mixture over 4 of the slices of toast. Top with the lettuce mixture and the avocado slices, and then with the other 4 slices of toast.

Cut the sandwiches in half on the diagonal and serve.

ROAST CHICKEN AND SCALLION SANDWICH
WITH WARM MAYONNAISE

Serves 4

Years of watching food costs in restaurants have left me attuned to every morsel in the fridge and how best to use it. After you've mastered the Perfect Roast Chicken on page 148, here's what you can do with the leftovers. Because you've made a sultry, moist bird, the sandwiches will be equally perfect.

There are no hard-and-fast rules beyond starting with a fantastic bird, good bread, and a luscious warm mayonnaise. From there, you can add radishes, watercress, tomatoes, egg, cheese, peppers, avocado, artichokes—be creative!

1 **lemon**	1 **1-pound ciabatta loaf**
1 **bunch scallions**	**Shredded meat from ½ roast**
1 **cup extra-virgin olive oil**	**chicken (see page 148;**
3 **large egg yolks**	**about 1½ cups meat)**
1 **teaspoon capers, drained**	1 **tablespoon chopped fresh chives**
Kosher salt and freshly ground	
black pepper	

Juice the lemon. Chop the scallions.

Pour the olive oil into a measuring cup or a pitcher with a narrow spout. In a double boiler or a stainless steel bowl set over a saucepan filled with an inch or two of simmering water, whisk together the lemon juice, egg yolks, and 1 tablespoon of the olive oil, then whisk for 3 minutes. Whisking, dribble in a few more teaspoons of the oil until the sauce begins to emulsify. Still whisking, slowly drizzle in the rest of the oil in a very thin stream—not too fast, or the mayonnaise will "break," or curdle—to form

a soft, fluffy mayonnaise. Remove from the heat and stir in the scallions and capers. Season with salt and pepper.

Heat the broiler. Split the ciabatta horizontally in half and toast it under the broiler.

Meanwhile, in a medium bowl, combine the chicken and mayonnaise. Season with salt and pepper to taste.

Spread the chicken mixture over the ciabatta halves. Cut the ciabatta into eight 3-inch-wide strips, sprinkle with the chives, and serve open-faced.

PULLED BEEF AND BBQ SAUCE SANDWICH
10 sandwiches

Here's an amazingly versatile recipe. You slow-braise a beef roast in beer redolent of onions, garlic, and chiles. Once the beef is cooked, it benefits from a two-day stay in the refrigerator. After its fridge holiday, you can use the beef for sandwiches, a taco filling, a base for chili, or a pasta sauce, or you could even top it with mashed potatoes for a beef shepherd's pie.

8   onions
8   garlic cloves
3   Anaheim chiles
8   pounds beef chuck for stew, cut into 2-inch chunks, or beef cheeks
    Kosher salt and freshly ground black pepper
¼   cup olive oil
4   12-ounce bottles lager

2   tablespoons chopped fresh flat-leaf parsley
1   sweet onion, such as Vidalia
4   canned Italian plum tomatoes, preferably San Marzano
¼   cup chopped fresh cilantro
1   tablespoon Worcestershire sauce
1   teaspoon Tabasco sauce
10 potato buns

Chop the onions. Mince the garlic. Stem, seed, and finely chop the chiles.

Season the beef well with salt and pepper. Heat 2 tablespoons of the olive oil in a large enameled cast-iron casserole or Dutch oven over medium-high heat. Add the beef, in batches, adding more oil as needed, and sear on all sides until browned, 10 to 15 minutes total. Transfer the beef to a bowl as it is browned.

Add the onions, garlic, and chiles to the casserole and sauté for 10 minutes, or until the onions are translucent. Pour in the beer and bring to a simmer, scraping up the browned bits on the bottom of the pot. Return the beef to the casserole. Add the parsley and 2 quarts water and bring just to a simmer. Cover with a tight-

fitting lid, reduce the heat, and simmer gently for 5 to 7 hours, stirring occasionally, until the beef is falling apart and has started to shred. (The beef should be made 1 to 2 days ahead, covered, and refrigerated.)

Scoop out 2 cups of the cooking liquid and set aside. Shred the beef with two forks. Dice the sweet onion. Place the onion, tomatoes, cilantro, reserved cooking liquid, Worcestershire, and Tabasco sauce in a blender and pulse to break up the tomatoes, then puree the mixture. Reheat the sauce if necessary.

Toast the buns. Place a bun bottom on each plate and top with a heap of the beef, then some of the sauce. Place the bun tops over the beef and serve.

GRILLED FONTINA AND PROSCIUTTO SANDWICH

4 sandwiches

The essence of a grilled cheese sandwich is melting cheese inside golden brown crusty bread. To achieve optimal results, you need the right cooking surface. I recommend a well-seasoned cast-iron skillet or flat griddle sauté pan.

A few years ago, the Italians achieved a culinary coup. They pestered the United States to allow the importation of real prosciutto from Parma. Thanks to their efforts, these beautiful hams, which are aged for at least nine months in salt only, have become fairly ubiquitous in our markets. They have a nutty, sweet texture that marries beautifully with the Fontina and cooked bread.

True raw-cow's-milk Fontina comes from the slopes of Mont Blanc in the Italian Alps. The rich soil, grasses, and mountain water all contribute to a perfect cheese.

½ pound sliced imported prosciutto
½ pound sliced Italian Fontina
8 slices country levain bread
(French sourdough)

About 8 tablespoons (1 stick)
unsalted butter, at room temperature
Cornichons, pickled peppers,
and good mustard, for serving

Layer the slices of prosciutto and Fontina, alternating them, on 4 of the bread slices. Top with the remaining bread and lightly butter the top of each sandwich.

Melt 1½ tablespoons of the remaining butter in a large skillet (use two pans to speed up the process, if you like). When the butter begins to bubble, add one sandwich, unbuttered side down, and cook, turning once, until the bread is golden brown on both sides and the cheese is beginning to ooze out. Place on a cutting board and cook the remaining sandwiches, adding more butter to the pan for each one.

Cut each sandwich in half, place on plates, and serve with cornichons, pickled peppers, and mustard.

BACON AND GRUYÈRE BURGER
WITH GUACAMOLE

4 burgers

A burger is a miraculous meal in any guise. I have fond memories of Bob's Big Boy in Reno. I was a seventeen-year-old trombonist, playing in rock bands and orchestras, and trying like hell to learn to play jazz. Bob's and A&W were the only meals I could afford. Bob's provided the luxury of table service—worth the extra 50 cents or so. And the twenty-five-year-old waitress who took a fancy to me was an added plus. The burger there wasn't great, but the ranch dressing was spectacular!

Today when it comes to burgers, I'm a purist. I want grass-fed ground chuck with 20 percent fat. I prefer to grind—or, rather, chop—my own meat. The rough, rustic quality of the meat creates a real bite.

A note on doneness: Simply put, time is fairly irrelevant when cooking meat. What is important is how to *perceive* doneness. Testing doneness can be as simple as using an instant-read thermometer. But your index finger is actually far more precise. You'll see chefs prodding the surfaces of meat, fish, or poultry with our fingers. What are we testing for? Every protein has a slightly different feel, and you learn through experience how to determine the level of doneness from how spongy the meat feels.

So, cook the burgers on the first side until they are crispy. Immediately flip them over and cook them for about 2 minutes longer. Gently touching the middle of one burger, push down quickly but firmly. With a burger, if there is no resiliency, the burger is rare. Take it off the heat if that's what you want. If the texture is slightly firmer, then it's medium-rare. Take it off at once. Meat retains heat and will distribute that surface heat throughout once off the heat. If you cook it a few minutes longer, you'll feel an almost rubber-ball resilience: your burger is medium. If you want your burger well-done, cook it until it does not give at all.

2½	pounds ground or chopped (see headnote) beef chuck, preferably grass-fed meat, 80/20 lean-to-fat ratio	2	ripe Hass avocados
	Kosher salt and freshly ground black pepper	2	tablespoons minced sweet onion, such as Vidalia
8	thick strips nitrate-free bacon, such as Niman Ranch	1	tablespoon olive oil
		1	very ripe large tomato
		¼	cup grated Gruyère cheese, preferably French cave-aged
		4	kaiser rolls, split

Prepare a medium grill fire, preferably using hardwood charcoal. (If it's winter or raining or you're just not in the mood, cook the burgers in a cast-iron skillet.)

Meanwhile, mix the beef with salt and pepper to taste and shape into 4 burgers. Set aside on a plate.

Cook the bacon in a cast-iron skillet over medium heat. Drain on paper towels.

Meanwhile, halve the avocados, and scoop out the flesh into a small bowl. Add the onion and olive oil and mash with the avocado. Cut the tomato into 4 slices.

Grill the burgers (or cook in the skillet over medium heat) until medium-rare. Top with the cheese and remove to a platter.

Lightly grill or toast the rolls. Place a burger on each bun bottom, top with guacamole and bacon, and lay a tomato slice over all. Cover with the bun tops and serve.

EGGPLANT, PEPPER, ZUCCHINI, AND PESTO SANDWICH

12 sandwiches

This is my favorite summer snack when eggplant is cheap and plentiful. You'll need to make a simple, rustic pizza dough. It takes all of 20 minutes, and it bakes into puffy, crisp breads. The pesto is very straightforward, and it, too, is a breeze to make.

This recipe was perfected during long, languorous days spent in the South of France with my two-year-old daughter. The local St.-Tropez and Grimaud markets were teeming with eggplants, tomatoes of all shapes and sizes, and bell peppers.

I would get up near dawn, pack up my snuggly, affectionate little daughter, and drive into the town of Grimaud. Perched on a hillside with beautiful plane trees was one of the greatest pastry shops in France, where Hannah and I would choose our pastries—always a croissant for me and a pain au chocolat for her—and settle in at a roadside table for our prebreakfast snack. The shop offered many specialties, among them a pissaladière topped with ratatouille. That was my inspiration for this scrumptious sandwich. Essentially, it's a deconstructed ratatouille, with the components layered rather than stewed together.

Dough

¼ cup lager

1 ¼-ounce package active dry yeast

3 cups unbleached all-purpose flour, preferably organic, plus more for kneading

2 tablespoons olive oil

1 cup whole wheat flour, preferably organic

1½ teaspoons sea salt

Pesto

¼ cup pine nuts

1 garlic clove

20 fresh basil leaves

¼ cup freshly grated Parmesan cheese

1 cup olive oil

Vegetable filling

½ pound zucchini

½ pound eggplant

1 small onion

2 garlic cloves

1 green bell pepper

4 medium tomatoes

2 tablespoons olive oil

MAKE THE DOUGH

Mix the beer, yeast, and 1 cup of the white flour in a large bowl. Add the oil and ½ cup warm water and mix with a wooden spoon for 3 minutes. Let this sponge rest, covered with plastic wrap, for 1 hour in a warm, draft-free spot. (The sponge can be made a day ahead; refrigerate after 1 hour, and bring to room temperature before proceeding.)

Stir the remaining 2 cups white flour, the whole wheat flour, and the salt into the sponge. Add 1 cup warm water and stir well. The dough should be moist; if it seems too dry, add a little more water.

Dust a work surface with white flour. Dump out the dough and knead for 3 to 4 minutes, or until smooth and elastic.

Wash and dry the bowl and oil it. Return the dough to the bowl, turning once to coat with oil. Cover and let rise until the dough is double its original size, about 2 hours.

MAKE THE PESTO

Heat the oven to 350 degrees.

Toast the pine nuts on a baking sheet in the oven, stirring occasionally, for about 5 minutes, until lightly toasted. Transfer to a food processor. Turn the oven to 400 degrees.

Add the garlic, basil, and Parmesan to the food processor and process to a rough paste. With the processor running, slowly pour the olive oil through the feed tube. Transfer the pesto to a bowl and cover it tightly with plastic.

SHAPE AND BAKE THE BREADS

Dust two baking sheets lightly with white flour. Return the dough to the floured work surface and cut it into 12 equal portions. Form each portion of dough into an oval and dust the tops with flour. Place them on baking sheets.

Bake the breads for 35 to 40 minutes, or until golden brown. They should make a nice thumping sound when you tap them. Remove the breads from the oven and let cool on racks for at least 10 minutes.

MEANWHILE, MAKE THE VEGETABLE FILLING

Dice the zucchini. Dice the eggplant. Dice the onion. Mince the garlic. Stem, seed, and dice the bell pepper. Core and dice the tomatoes.

Heat the olive oil in a large heavy skillet over medium-high heat until almost smoking. Add the zucchini, eggplant, and onion and cook, stirring, until golden brown, about 10 minutes. Add the garlic and bell pepper, reduce the heat to medium, and cook for 20 minutes. Add the tomatoes and cook for 5 minutes. Remove from the heat. Allow the mixture to cool. Stir in the pesto.

Make a pocket in each bread, slicing into one of the longer sides. Fill each one with a good helping of the eggplant mixture and serve.

NOTE: If you are not serving a crowd, store the extra filling, covered, in the refrigerator. Bring to room temperature before stuffing the breads.

PIZZA WITH BACON, SCALLIONS, PARMESAN, AND TOMATO

Two 12-inch pizzas

My editor, Rux Martin, likes pizza—well, she likes my pizza! When guests come to my house for dinner, this is the one I invariably serve. Scallions are scrumptious here, oniony without being intrusive, slightly crunchy, and a terrific foil for the bacon and cheese. Use real Parmigiano-Reggiano from Parma. Pregrated domestic Parmesan doesn't cut it. As for the tomatoes: here is a dilemma. Yes, fresh are preferred, but great tomatoes are hard to get out of season. Canned San Marzanos, drained and diced, will work very well.

4   cups unbleached all-purpose flour, preferably organic, plus extra for rolling
1   tablespoon honey
¼   cup olive oil
1   ¼-ounce package active dry yeast
    Sea salt

¼   pound thick-cut bacon
1   bunch scallions
4   medium ripe tomatoes (see headnote)
¼   cup freshly grated fresh Parmigiano-Reggiano
    Freshly ground black pepper

In a large bowl, combine 1 cup of the flour, the honey, 2 cups warm water, 2 tablespoons of the olive oil, and the yeast. Mix well. Let this sponge sit in a warm, draft-free spot for 1 hour, or until doubled.

With a wooden spoon, stir the remaining 3 cups flour and 2 teaspoons salt into the sponge. Knead for 10 minutes in the bowl or transfer to the counter and knead, adding a little more warm water if necessary; the dough should be moist, not dry. Cover with plastic wrap and let rise for 1½ to 2 hours, until doubled in size.

Position a rack in the lower third of the oven and heat the oven to 450 degrees. If you have a pizza stone, place it on the oven rack to preheat for 30 minutes. If not using a stone, lightly oil two pizza pans or baking sheets.

Dice the bacon. Slice the scallions. Core and dice the tomatoes.

Divide the dough in half. Roll out one piece of dough on a lightly floured surface to a 12-inch round. If using a pizza stone, dust a baker's peel (or a rimless baking sheet) with flour and place the dough on it. Sprinkle with half the bacon, half the scallions, half the tomatoes, and 2 tablespoons of the Parmesan. Drizzle with a tablespoon of olive oil, sprinkle with salt and pepper, and slide the dough onto the hot stone.

Alternatively, place the dough on one of the oiled pizza pans or baking sheets, add the toppings, and place the pan in the oven.

Bake until the crust is golden brown, 10 to 12 minutes. Meanwhile, assemble the remaining pizza.

Cut the baked pizza into wedges and serve hot. Bake the remaining pizza and serve.

PASTA

HANDMADE PASTA IS MOST SUITABLE FOR DELICATE SAUCES, WHILE MACHINE-MADE DRIED PASTA IS BETTER FOR STURDIER DISHES.

The flourishing Italian community in San Francisco has given rise to many small trattorias that adhere ferociously to authenticity. It was at these restaurants that I first sampled delicate angel hair pasta, delicious hearty pappardelle, and beautiful baked pastas.

These trattorias inspired me to try my own hand at pasta making. I gingerly stepped up to a mound of flour and began. I soon discovered that handmade pasta is most suitable for delicate sauces, while machine-made dried pasta is better for sturdier dishes.

I started to combine sauces for fish or poultry, adding grilled items, and cooking the pasta just until al dente. My approach was to combine three or four simple items, such as grilled fresh scallops, a light cream sauce, and fresh egg noodles. This type of cooking eventually came to be known as "California style."

My basic pasta dough uses large egg yolks, organic unbleached all-purpose flour, and a little salt. You can make the dough using either a food processor or your hands, then rolling it out by hand or with a hand-cranked machine. The result is toothsome, luxurious pasta.

PASTA

TAGLIATELLE
WITH BEETS
AND CREAM

TAGLIATELLE
WITH BEETS AND CREAM

6 first-course servings or 4 main-course servings

This is an intensely flavored and dramatic dish, with its high-contrast presentation of china-white pasta and brightly colored beets. The vegetables require a little finesse, but with a bit of practice, you'll be cutting like a pro. Try to make the portions small, so as not to overwhelm your guests. I served this dish as an appetizer at an extremely elaborate food and wine function, and it was the most popular item of the evening. You can use 1 pound dried angel hair pasta instead of the homemade tagliatelle and the dish will still be excellent.

Pasta
- 6 large egg yolks
- 2 cups unbleached all-purpose flour
- ½ teaspoon kosher salt

Beets and cream
- 2 medium beets
- 1 leek

- 2 celery stalks
- 2 medium carrots
- 1 medium celery root
- 1 red bell pepper
- 3 tablespoons unsalted butter
- 1 cup heavy cream
  Kosher salt and freshly ground
  black pepper

MAKE THE PASTA

Place the egg yolks, flour, and salt in a food processor and pulse just until a ball of dough forms. Transfer the pasta to a floured work surface and knead it for 10 minutes. Let the pasta rest, covered with plastic wrap, for 1 hour. Divide the pasta dough into 4 pieces. Work with one piece of dough at a time, keeping the rest covered. Using a pasta machine, roll out each piece through each setting from the widest to the next-to-thinnest, and lay the sheets of dough on a lightly floured surface.

Using the pasta cutters, cut each sheet into ¼-inch-wide strips. Spread the pasta out on the floured surface and let dry for 1 hour. (Once it is thoroughly dry, the pasta can be refrigerated in a plastic bag for up to 1 day or frozen for up to 1 month.)

Trim the beets. Put them in a medium saucepan, add water to cover, and bring to a simmer. Simmer for 45 minutes to 1 hour, or until tender.

Drain the beets, reserving the cooking liquid. Let the beets cool, then peel them and cut into fine julienne strips. Set aside.

Meanwhile, cut off the leek's root and the dark green parts, leaving about 6 inches. Cut the leek lengthwise in half and wash carefully. Slice into fine julienne strips. Unless the celery is very young, it will need to be peeled. Remove the tough strings with a vegetable peeler or paring knife, then cut the celery into 2-inch-long julienne strips. Peel the carrots and slice the same way. Peel the celery root with a paring knife and cut into julienne. Stem and seed the pepper. Cut away the inner ribs, then cut it into very thin strips.

Bring a small saucepan of water (no salt) to a boil. Add the leek strips and cook until just crisp-tender, then lift them out with a slotted spoon and drain on paper towels. One by one, blanch the celery, carrots, celery root, and bell pepper until crisp-tender.

Bring a large pot of salted water to a boil.

Melt 2 tablespoons of the butter in a large saucepan. Add the vegetables and cook for 2 minutes. Add the cream and bring to a boil. Season with salt and pepper and turn off the heat.

Meanwhile, cook the pasta in the boiling water for about 2 minutes, until just tender.

Drain the pasta and toss it with the vegetables, adding the remaining tablespoon butter and 2 tablespoons of the beet cooking liquid or more as needed if the pasta seems dry. Taste for seasoning, adding salt and pepper if needed, and serve.

FETTUCCINE WITH CREMINI MUSHROOMS
AND ONION MARMALADE

8 first-course servings or 4 main-course servings

Cremini mushrooms are simply young portobello mushrooms. There is a goofy notion out there that one should not wash mushrooms. In truth, what happens in the forest? Doesn't it rain? Here I ask you to thoroughly submerge these mushrooms to remove any grit and sand. This will ensure that there are no surprises in the pasta sauce.

The marmalade is a savory one, with no sugar. It uses red wine as a flavoring agent. When cooking the marmalade, don't reduce it too much, or it won't stick to the noodles.

Onion marmalade

- 2 red onions
- 4 tablespoons (½ stick) unsalted butter
  Kosher salt and freshly ground
    black pepper
- ½ cup Pinot Noir
- ½ cup chopped mixed fresh herbs
    (rosemary, thyme, sage, and
    parsley)

Fettuccine

- 2½ pounds cremini mushrooms
- 4 garlic cloves
- 4 tablespoons (½ stick) unsalted butter
  Kosher salt and freshly ground
    black pepper
- 1 tablespoon fino (dry) sherry
- 1½ pounds dried fettuccine

MAKE THE MARMALADE

Slice the onions crosswise into thin slices. Melt the butter in a large heavy saucepan over medium-low heat. Add the onions, season with salt and pepper to taste, and cook for about 20 minutes, stirring every 5 minutes, until very soft and caramelized.

Add the wine, reduce the heat to low, and cook the onions, stirring often, for another 20 minutes, or until the wine has reduced to a slightly sticky glaze. Add the herbs and stir well. Turn off the heat and cover to keep warm.

MAKE THE FETTUCCINE

Put a large pot of salted water on to boil.

Submerge the mushrooms in a bowl of cold water and let stand for a few minutes, then lift out the mushrooms, drain on paper towels, and pat dry. Trim and halve the mushrooms. Mince the garlic. Melt the butter in a large deep skillet over medium heat. Add the garlic and cook, stirring, until lightly colored. Toss in the mushrooms, add salt and pepper to taste, and cook gently for 5 minutes, or until the mushrooms have exuded a little liquid. Add

the sherry, cover, and cook for 2 to 3 minutes. When the mushrooms are flavorful but still firm, turn off the heat.

Add the pasta to the boiling water and cook according to the instructions on the package until al dente. Drain the pasta, reserving ½ cup of the cooking water.

Meanwhile, reheat the marmalade. Add the pasta and the reserved cooking water to the marmalade and toss well. Divide the pasta among serving plates. Top with the mushroom mixture and a good sprinkling of black pepper. Serve at once.

PASTA WITH ASPARAGUS

6 first-course servings or 4 main-course servings

This dish captures the essence of spring. The best approach to asparagus is one of simplicity. The spears should be cooked just right, not too crunchy or too limp. The garnish of crunchy bread crumbs contrasts with the silky pasta and sauce.

1 pound pencil-thin asparagus	½ cup fresh bread crumbs
1 pound cherry tomatoes	1 pound orecchiette or fusilli
3 garlic cloves	2 tablespoons unsalted butter
20 fresh basil leaves	1 cup grated Italian Fontina cheese
3 tablespoons olive oil	(about 4 ounces)
Kosher salt and freshly ground black pepper	

Heat the oven to 350 degrees.

Put a large pot of salted water on to boil.

Holding a spear of asparagus by its tip and tail, bring the ends together: the bottom will snap off at the part where its bitterness ends. Trim the rest of the asparagus to approximately the same length. Cut the stalks into ½-inch pieces. Halve the tomatoes. Mince the garlic. Julienne the basil.

Heat the olive oil in a large skillet over medium heat. Add the garlic and sauté for 2 minutes. Add the tomatoes and asparagus and cook, stirring occasionally, until the asparagus is tender, 8 to 10 minutes. Season with salt and 1 tablespoon pepper, turn off the heat, and cover to keep warm.

Meanwhile, spread the bread crumbs on a small baking sheet and toast in the oven, stirring occasionally, for 8 to 10 minutes, or until golden. Set aside.

Cook the pasta in the boiling water according to the instructions on the package until al dente. Drain, reserving about 1 cup of the cooking water.

Just before the pasta is done, reheat the asparagus mixture over low heat. Add the butter. Toss the pasta with the asparagus mixture, adding small ladlefuls of the pasta cooking water as necessary if the pasta seems dry. Add the basil and toss quickly, then add the cheese. When the cheese has just melted, scatter over the bread crumbs and toss again. Taste for seasoning, adding salt and more pepper if needed, and serve promptly.

LINGUINE WITH SOFT-SHELL CRABS

4 first-course servings or 2 main-course servings

Soft-shell crabs are the star crustacean of springtime, and they show up well into summer, when the corn gets going. The recipe uses little butter and no cream, yet it tastes rich and luxurious. Have the fishmonger clean the crabs if you prefer, and then cook them as soon as possible.

4	live soft-shell crabs or 8 ounces lump crabmeat	1–4	tablespoons olive oil Kosher salt and freshly ground black pepper
2	red onions	½	pound dried linguine
4	ears corn	12	fresh basil leaves
3	large ripe tomatoes		Fresh thyme leaves, for garnish
2	tablespoons unsalted butter		

Clean the crabs if necessary, following the instructions on page 102. Cover and refrigerate the crabs until ready to cook them.

Put a large pot of salted water on to boil.

Slice the onions. Husk the corn and cut the kernels off the corncobs. Core and dice the tomatoes.

Heat the butter and 1 tablespoon of the oil in a large skillet over medium heat. Add the onions and cook, stirring, until softened, about 10 minutes. Add the corn and tomatoes and cook, stirring, for about 3 minutes to heat through. Season with salt and pepper. If using lump crabmeat, stir it in now.

If using soft-shells, transfer the onion-tomato mixture to a bowl. Wipe out the skillet, pour in the remaining 3 tablespoons olive oil, and heat over medium heat. Pat the crabs dry and add them, shell side down, to the pan. Cook, covered, until golden on the first side. Flip the crabs and cook them, covered, for 5 minutes longer. Add the onion-tomato mixture to the pan.

Meanwhile, cook the linguine in the boiling water according to the package directions until al dente.

Chop the basil leaves.

Drain the pasta and add to the skillet with the crab. Toss well, then add the basil and salt and pepper to taste and toss again. Serve hot, garnished with the thyme.

SEA SCALLOP FETTUCCINE
4 first-course servings or 2 main-course servings

One night when I was chef at Michael's in Santa Monica, a customer brought in some very valuable old white Burgundies. I needed a dish that would complement the magnificent wine, setting it off without competing with it or being overly shy. I quickly rolled out some pasta, made a sauce from some scallop scraps, and concocted the following recipe. Later, at Jams, I perfected the dish when a supplier brought me a chest filled with squeaky-clean, glistening, huge Maine scallops. They had been handpicked from the sea that morning by divers. I grilled those gorgeous fat beauties over charcoal, tossed them with a light, lemony cream sauce, and paired them with fresh pasta. Overnight, it became one of my signature dishes.

Pasta

4 large egg yolks

1 cup unbleached all-purpose flour

½ teaspoon kosher salt

1 pound sea scallops

1 shallot or small onion

1 Meyer lemon or regular lemon

4 fresh parsley sprigs

1 cup dry white wine

⅔ cup heavy cream

1 tablespoon olive oil, plus more
for the scallops

Kosher salt and freshly ground
black pepper

MAKE THE PASTA

Place the egg yolks, flour, and salt in a food processor and pulse just until a ball of dough forms. Transfer the dough to a floured work surface and knead for 10 minutes. Let the pasta rest, covered with plastic wrap, for 15 minutes.

Divide the pasta dough into 3 pieces. Work with one piece of dough at a time, keeping the rest covered. Using a pasta machine, roll out each piece through each setting from the widest to the next-to-thinnest setting. Dust each sheet of

pasta with flour and stack on top of one another on a countertop dusted with flour and let dry for 5 minutes.

Cut the pasta into ¼-inch-wide strips by putting it through the fettuccine cutters on the pasta machine. Toss the fettuccine with flour, spread it out on the floured surface, and let dry for 1 hour. (Once it is thoroughly dry, the pasta can be refrigerated in a plastic bag for up to 1 day or frozen for up to 1 month.)

Bring a large pot of salted water to a boil.

Clean the scallops by removing the tough muscle from the side of each one; reserve the muscles. Slice the shallot or onion. Juice the lemon and set the juice aside. Place the scallop muscles, shallot or onion, parsley, and wine in a small saucepan and bring to a simmer over medium heat. Lower the heat and simmer gently for 10 minutes.

Strain the liquid, return it to the saucepan, and boil to reduce to ¼ cup. Add the cream and simmer for 5 minutes, or until thickened. Remove from the heat.

Rub the scallops with olive oil and season with salt and pepper on both sides. Heat the tablespoon of olive oil in a large heavy skillet over medium-high heat. Add the scallops in a single layer and cook for 3 minutes on each side, or until golden brown. Remove the scallops to a plate and set aside, loosely covered to keep warm. Pour the cream sauce into the skillet and keep warm over very low heat.

Drop the pasta into the boiling water and boil for 2 minutes, or until just tender. Drain and add to the sauce in the skillet, along with any juices from the scallop plate. Season with the lemon juice and salt and pepper, and toss the pasta with the sauce.

Transfer the pasta to a hot platter, decorate with the scallops, and serve immediately.

WHOLE WHEAT SPAGHETTI
WITH SPICY CLAMS

6 first-course servings or 4 main-course servings

Whole wheat spaghetti makes a great contrast to the sweetness of the clams. Manila clams are wonderfully sweet, small white-fleshed clams. Since they are raised near river outlets and estuaries, where the saline content is lower than that of the open sea, they are usually not very salty. Their meat is creamy and toothsome and blends well with spicy ingredients. The cooking time for the clams is brief—don't overcook them!

1½ pounds Manila clams or cherrystones
2 red tomatoes
1 yellow tomato (or use all red
        tomatoes)
1 red bell pepper
1 yellow bell pepper
4 garlic cloves
1 cup dry white wine

1 teaspoon red pepper flakes
1 pound dried whole wheat spaghetti
4 tablespoons (½ stick) unsalted butter
½ cup pitted oil- or brine-cured
        black olives from Italy
8 fresh tarragon leaves (optional)
    Kosher salt and freshly ground
        black pepper

Put a large pot of salted water on to boil.

Scrub the clams under cold running water and rinse well. Drain, place in a bowl, and refrigerate.

Core and coarsely chop the tomatoes. Stem and seed the peppers and finely mince them. Smash and peel the garlic cloves.

Combine the wine and red pepper flakes in a small saucepan, bring to a simmer, and simmer, covered, for 10 minutes on low.

Cook the spaghetti in the boiling water according to the package instructions until al dente.

Meanwhile, place a large deep skillet over high heat, add the clams, garlic, and the wine mixture, cover, and bring to a boil. Cook just until the clams open, 2 to 3 minutes. Discard any that haven't opened.

Add the butter, tomatoes, peppers, olives, and tarragon, if using, to the pan. Cover and bring to a simmer. Season carefully with salt, since the clams may be salty, and pepper.

Drain the pasta and toss well with the clam sauce. Serve right away.

FETTUCCINE WITH CALAMARI AND SUMMER SQUASH

6 first-course servings or 4 main-course servings

In this dish, slightly crunchy summer squash, sweet onions, and squid combine with flavored noodles. Flavored pasta is beautiful and festive, and readily available. The most colorful types are spinach and red bell pepper noodles. You can find dried versions at www.deciopasta.com or at your local market. Fresh egg pasta made with spinach, red pepper, or even beets is available at www.rossipasta.com. If you like, you can use just 1 pound dried spinach fettuccine, also; De Cecco is a good, readily available brand.

2 sweet onions, such as Vidalia	1 tablespoon fresh thyme leaves
4 ears corn	Kosher salt and freshly ground
1 pound zucchini	black pepper
1 pound yellow squash	½ pound dried spinach fettuccine
2 pounds squid or 12 ounces	(see headnote)
cleaned squid	½ pound dried or fresh beet, red pepper,
¼ cup extra-virgin olive oil	or tomato fettuccine
¼ cup champagne vinegar	
or rice wine vinegar	

Put a large pot of salted water on to boil.

Thinly slice the onions. Husk the corn and slice off the kernels with a sharp knife. Julienne the zucchini and squash. If necessary, clean the squid (see page 39). Cut into ¼-inch-wide rings; set aside.

Heat 2 tablespoons of the oil in a large skillet over medium-high heat. Add the onions and sauté for 2 minutes, or until softened. Add the zucchini, squash, and corn and sauté for 3 minutes. Stir in the vinegar and thyme and heat briefly. Transfer the squash mixture to a bowl and wipe out the skillet with a paper towel.

Add the remaining 2 tablespoons oil to the pan and heat over medium-high heat. Add the squid and sauté for 30 seconds; return the squash mixture to the skillet. Stir well and season with salt and pepper. Turn off the heat and cover to keep warm.

Meanwhile, add the pasta to the boiling water and cook according to the package instructions, until al dente. Drain.

Toss the pasta with the squid mixture and serve immediately.

LASAGNA WITH SMOKED HAM AND CABBAGE

8 main-course servings

I spent my fortieth birthday weekend hedonistically in eastern Italy. On the day itself, an Italian friend insisted that we come to her hometown of Bologna. There, at Diana, probably the most traditional of the restaurants in the town center, we were served a typical Emilia-Romagna first course of pasta. It was a winter dish, lasagna layered with mozzarella, Parmesan, butter, ham, and cabbage. The ingredients are ordinary; the magic is in how they speak to each other.

Pasta

1 small bunch spinach (about 2 cups loosely packed leaves)

10 fresh basil leaves

3 large egg yolks

1 cup unbleached all-purpose flour

½ teaspoon kosher salt

2 medium onions

4 garlic cloves

8 shallots

2 red bell peppers

3 tablespoons olive oil

Kosher salt and freshly ground black pepper

1½ cups shredded napa cabbage

2 tablespoons minced peeled fresh ginger

8 ounces sliced good ham, such as Applegate or Boar's Head

6 tablespoons (¾ stick) unsalted butter, plus more for the baking dish

6 tablespoons freshly grated Parmigiano-Reggiano cheese

8 ounces mozzarella cheese, shredded

MAKE THE PASTA

Wash and stem the spinach. Blanch the spinach and basil in a pot of boiling water; remove after a second or two. Drain and let cool.

Puree the spinach and basil with the egg yolks in a food processor. Add the flour and salt and pulse just until a ball of dough forms; you may need to add a little water to help the process along. Transfer the dough to a floured work surface and knead for 2 minutes. Let it rest, covered with plastic wrap, for 15 minutes.

Divide the dough into 2 pieces. Work with one piece at a time, keeping the rest covered. Using a pasta machine, roll each piece through each setting from the widest to the next-to-thinnest, and lay the sheets on a floured surface. Cut the sheets into 5-x-10-inch lasagna noodles. Toss them with flour and spread out on the work surface.

Put a large pot of salted water on to boil.

Thinly slice the onions, garlic, and shallots. Stem, seed, and finely chop the peppers. Heat the olive oil in a large skillet over medium heat. Add the onions, garlic, shallots, and salt and pepper to taste and cook for 10 minutes, or until the onions are tender. Add the peppers to the onion mixture and sauté just until tender. Remove from the heat.

Add the cabbage to the onion mixture, along with the ginger. Slice the ham into thin strips and stir it into the cabbage mixture. Taste for seasoning, adding more salt and pepper if needed.

Cook the noodles in the boiling water for 3 minutes, or until slightly tender. Drain and immerse in a large bowl of cold water.

Preheat the oven to 350 degrees. Generously butter a 10-x-12-inch or similar-sized baking pan.

Sprinkle about 1 tablespoon of the grated Parmesan cheese over the bottom of the baking pan. Cover the bottom of the pan with a single layer of noodles. Sprinkle with one third of the cabbage mixture, dot with 2 tablespoons of the butter, and sprinkle with 1 tablespoon of the Parmesan and then one third of the mozzarella cheese. Repeat the layering 2 times, with a layer of noodles, one third of the cabbage, 2 tablespoons of the butter, 1 tablespoon of the Parmesan, and one third of the mozzarella, finishing with a layer of noodles. Sprinkle with the remaining 2 tablespoons Parmesan cheese. (If you don't have enough pasta for a final layer, just sprinkle with the cheese.)

Bake until golden brown and bubbly, 15 to 20 minutes. Let stand for 5 to 10 minutes before serving.

MY EARLIEST
MEMORIES ARE OF
MY GRANDMOTHER
POLISHING EGGS,
A BANDANA TIED
AROUND HER HEAD,
AND MY GRANDFATHER,
THOUGH LEGALLY
BLIND, SCURRYING
AROUND TO GATHER
EGGS AND FEED THE
CHICKENS.

POULTRY

In the 1940s, tiring of New York City, my grandparents moved to the rustic town of Cotati in Sonoma County, California, to raise chickens. My two great-uncles and a few other New Yorkers soon followed. This strange collection of city-gone-country farmers was a culturally diverse lot; probably the only common denominator among them was their chicken farms. My earliest memories are of my grandmother polishing eggs, a bandana tied around her head, and my grandfather, though legally blind, scurrying around to gather eggs and feed the chickens, and then rushing off to the county fair to purchase newly hatched chicks in order to replenish the stock.

Much has been said about how chickens should be raised and what varieties are the best. France has its *poulet fermier* (farmhouse chicken); England has its "free-ranging" chickens. Each variety of chicken tastes different. The best and most expensive chickens in the world are the purple-legged *poulets de Bresse* from the rich countryside of France near Lyon. But one thing is for sure: the average American has access to much better chicken now than ever before.

I try to use farm, not factory, chickens raised in as natural a situation as possible. The recipes in this chapter were tested with New York State free-range chickens or the California equivalent. My advice is to buy chicken from a butcher, not prepackaged at the supermarket. In many areas, free-range, corn-fed, or naturally raised chickens are becoming available. Ask for the freshest corn-fed chickens farmed without artificial feed. Try to find large fryer chickens, weighing at least 3½ to 4 pounds; the smaller ones are less flavorful. Kosher birds are also great. But these recipes will transform even an ordinary chicken into an extraordinary one.

POULTRY

Love of game birds—pheasant, duck, squab, and grouse—came rather late in my culinary adventures, probably because the only ones I had seen were in pictures or in recipes. At one time, America was overrun by wild turkey, pheasant, guinea fowl, prairie chickens, and quail, and these were a mainstay of the American diet. Game cookery is the glory of all cooking, and recently we've seen the birth of a new and growing cottage industry determined to raise game in natural environments. The taste of domestically raised squab and quail is almost as interesting as that of their wild varieties, and a few culinary tricks help considerably.

To locate game, start at your local butcher. Try to find poultry farms in your vicinity, since they not only raise better-tasting chickens but also sometimes stock game. If your family or friends hunt, so much the better. If they hit their limit and have a few to spare, invite them over to devour their bounty.

CHICKEN BREASTS WITH POBLANO CHILES

4 servings

This dish, which I created at my restaurant Bud's in Manhattan, features Southwestern flavors: poblano chiles, goat cheese, and a mixture of beans. Among the kitchen crew then was a young, good-looking Irish-American named Bobby Flay. This dish may have put some playful ideas into Bobby's head. Later he surprised us all by creating the pivotal Southwestern restaurant Mesa Grill.

The chicken breasts can be stuffed and refrigerated for up to a day before cooking, if you wish, or they can be cooked ahead of time and served cold or at room temperature. The ham bone adds a lot of salt, so add salt sparingly.

¼ cup each dried black, kidney, navy, and cannellini beans	Kosher salt and freshly ground black pepper
1 garlic head	4 large chicken breasts, 6–8 ounces each, skin on, bone-in or partially boned, with just the wing joint attached
4 fresh cilantro sprigs	
1 ham bone or ham hock	
1 bouquet garni (see page 5)	6 tablespoons olive oil
2 poblano chiles	2 teaspoons white wine vinegar
3 ounces soft fresh goat cheese	1 shallot
4 tablespoons (½ stick) unsalted butter, at room temperature	2 tablespoons sherry vinegar
	4–5 cups loosely packed torn mixed lettuces (frisée, red oak, Bibb, arugula)
2 fresh tarragon sprigs	
1 small bunch fresh chives	1 tablespoon fresh lemon juice

Pick over the beans and remove any stones or debris. Put in a medium bowl, cover with water, and soak for at least 8 hours, or overnight.

Separate the garlic cloves and peel them. Remove the leaves from the cilantro sprigs, reserving the stems; cover and refrigerate the leaves. Drain the beans, put them in a large saucepan, and add 2 quarts cold water, the ham bone or hock, garlic, bouquet garni, and cilantro stems. Bring to a simmer and cook, skimming any foam, until tender, about 2 hours. Drain the beans and let cool.

Meanwhile, roast the poblanos over medium-high heat on the stovetop or under a hot broiler, turning occasionally until they are blackened and blistered all over. Place them in a small bowl, cover with plastic wrap, and let them steam for 15 minutes.

Peel the peppers with your fingers (do not rinse) and stem and seed them. Finely dice them.

Crumble the goat cheese into a medium bowl. Add 2 tablespoons of the butter and half the diced poblanos and blend well. Remove the leaves from the tarragon sprigs and chop the tarragon, chives, and the reserved cilantro leaves. Add the tarragon, chives, and cilantro to the cheese mixture and mix again thoroughly. Season to taste with salt and pepper.

Lift the skin of one chicken breast and gently pull it back toward the wing (or where the wing was). Cut a ½-inch-deep 3-inch-long slit in the middle of the breast. Open this slit up a little, as you would squeeze open a baked potato, and salt and pepper the flesh. Spoon one quarter of the goat cheese mixture into the slit. It will overflow, but the skin will hold the mixture against the flesh. Pull the skin back over the stuffing. Repeat until all the breasts are stuffed. (The chicken breasts can be stuffed up to 1 day ahead, covered, and refrigerated. Bring to room temperature before proceeding.)

Place the cooled beans in a bowl and lightly toss them with 2 tablespoons of the olive oil, the white wine vinegar, and a judicious amount of salt and pepper.

Heat the broiler to low if possible or place the rack 4 to 6 inches from the heat. Place the chicken breasts skin side up on the broiler pan. Drizzle them with 2 tablespoons of the olive oil and salt and pepper them. Broil them until the skin is crisp and the chicken is cooked through, 15 to 20 minutes; an instant-read thermometer inserted into the thickest part of a breast should register 165 degrees. Check the chicken periodically to ensure that the skin doesn't burn. Transfer to a platter and cover to keep warm.

Mince the shallot. Add the shallot and any juices from the chicken to the bowl with the beans. Add the remaining diced poblanos, the remaining 2 tablespoons olive oil, and the sherry vinegar and toss well.

Place the lettuces in a large bowl, add the bean mixture, and toss well. Transfer the salad to a large platter.

Melt the remaining 2 tablespoons butter in a small skillet and cook until golden. Stir in the lemon juice and salt and pepper to taste.

Arrange the warm chicken breasts on top of the salad, drizzle the butter mixture over each chicken breast, and serve.

GRILLED (OR BROILED) CHICKEN

4 servings

When I moved to New York and opened Jams, I was the lone California chef in town, with my charcoal grill and long hair. My signature dish was half a grilled free-range chicken and a massive amount of perfectly crisp French fries on a huge plate. The dish has become my culinary anthem. What could be better to serve to royalty and commoners alike?

Here is my method: First, buy a good bird. Second, whether you grill or use a broiler, follow the directions carefully. Third, serve the bird hot! In the restaurant, I always fully boned the chickens, but that's a bit much to ask of a home cook, so instead I've given instructions here for butterflying the chicken.

The grill must be hot enough to cook the chicken but not so hot that it chars the bird. You want to make use of the fat that rests beneath the skin. The fat literally boils while the bird grills, causing the skin to crisp. This effect is called blistering (though most professional cooks are never taught this). Keep in mind, too, that free-range chickens have tougher, more resilient skin than supermarket chickens.

Serve with JW Fries (page 243) and salad.

1 3½- to 4-pound free-range, corn-fed, or naturally raised chicken
   Kosher salt and freshly ground black pepper
2 tablespoons olive oil (if broiling the chicken)

2 tablespoons unsalted butter
1 tablespoon chopped fresh herbs, such as rosemary, thyme, and parsley—whatever's available

Soak the chicken for 5 minutes in a large bowl filled with warm water to cover, to relax the flesh. Drain and dry the bird thoroughly with paper towels.

Butterfly the chicken by cutting down both sides of the backbone with poultry shears or sharp heavy scissors and removing the backbone (freeze it to use for stock). Open out the bird,

place it skin side up on the cutting board, and press down firmly with the palms of your hands to flatten the bird as much as you can. Pat dry again.

TO GRILL THE CHICKEN
Prepare a fire in a kettle grill, such as a Weber. Fill a chimney starter all the way to the top with hardwood charcoal. Light the chimney as usual.

When the coals are white, dump them out and place the grate over the coals. Wait for 10 minutes.

It is important to begin grilling the chicken with the skin side down—if not, the skin will not crisp well. Liberally salt and pepper the chicken and place it skin side down in the middle of the grill. Cover immediately and open the vent holes in the lid. Grill for 3 minutes, then turn the chicken 90 degrees, still skin side down, to create crosshatched grill marks on the skin. Cover the grill again and cook the chicken without moving it for an additional 6 minutes.

Turn the chicken over, cover, and grill until cooked through, about 15 minutes; an instant-read thermometer inserted in the thickest part of the thigh should register 165 degrees. (Or you can move the chicken off the direct heat to cook more slowly and give you time to make any accompanying dishes.)

TO BROIL THE CHICKEN

Heat the broiler. Rub the chicken with the olive oil, season well with salt and pepper, and place it skin side up in a shallow baking pan.

Place the pan under the broiler 4 inches from the heat source and cook until the skin is perfectly golden brown, 12 to 15 minutes. Turn the chicken over and cook for 5 minutes. Then turn the chicken skin side up again and cook until the skin is really crispy and an instant-read

thermometer inserted in the thickest part of the thigh registers 165 degrees.

Just before serving, melt the butter in a small skillet and stir in the chopped herbs, along with a little salt and pepper.

Quarter the chicken. Place on a platter, drizzle the herb butter over it, and serve right away.

BRICK CHICKEN WITH ROSÉ WINE,
PEAS, AND BACON

2 to 4 servings

The Tuscans developed a superior way to cook poultry, especially chicken. A butterflied and flattened whole bird is coated with salt and pepper, then cooked skin side down, weighed down with a brick, in butter and olive oil. (A foil-wrapped cast-iron skillet works fine as a stand-in for the brick.) The result is a fabulously succulent, moist bird with unbelievably crispy skin.

I alter the process slightly, by first cooking some bacon in the skillet, then cooking the chicken skin side down in the bacon fat to brown it (using that brick!) and finishing by braising it in a liberal splashing of rosé wine.

Fresh peas, shucked at the last minute so they remain crunchy and flavorful, are cooked with the bacon in herbs and butter. (Good frozen peas can be used if necessary.) The resulting sauce is vibrant with the flavors of smoky bacon, herbs, and rosé wine.

1 2½- to 3-pound free-range, corn-fed, or naturally raised chicken
3 tablespoons olive oil
   Kosher salt and freshly ground black pepper
1 cup diced smoky bacon
1 cup Bonnie Doon rosé wine or a similar good but inexpensive rosé

2 cups fresh peas (shucked at the last possible moment) or frozen peas, thawed
2 teaspoons chopped fresh marjoram, thyme, or sage
2 tablespoons unsalted butter

Butterfly the chicken by cutting down both sides of the backbone with poultry shears or sharp heavy scissors and removing the backbone (freeze it to use for stock). Open out the bird, place it skin side up on the cutting board, and press down firmly with the palms of your hands to flatten the bird as much as you can. Pat dry. Rub the chicken with 1 tablespoon of the olive oil. Rub salt all over the bird, then rub with pepper. Set aside on a plate.

Put the bacon and the remaining 2 tablespoons olive oil in an enameled cast-iron casserole or a Dutch oven and cook over medium heat until the bacon is just golden. Remove the bacon with a slotted spoon and drain on paper towels.

Carefully add the chicken to the pot, skin side down. Place a foil-wrapped brick (see headnote) on the chicken to press it against the hot pan and cook until golden brown, about 15 minutes. Remove the brick. Pour in the rosé and bring to a boil. Cook until the chicken is cooked through, about 15 minutes.

Meanwhile, just before the chicken is done, rinse the fresh peas with cold water.

Remove the chicken from the pot and, using the (clean) shears or scissors or a sharp knife, cut it into 4 or 8 pieces. Return the chicken to the pot.

Stir the peas, bacon, herbs, and butter into the pot and cook over medium heat to blend the flavors. Serve hot.

PERFECT ROAST CHICKEN
WITH MASHED POTATOES AND SPINACH

4 servings

Anyone can produce a perfect roast chicken. Most important, your chicken must have a good pedigree. Then it is a crucial factor that your oven is accurately calibrated. The only remaining step of importance is to baste the bird every 5 minutes or so.

While timing is not absolutely critical, I find that 10 minutes per pound (giblets and excess fat removed) is the right cooking time. For example, a 3½-pound bird takes only 35 to 40 minutes. Please remember that this is for oven time only—not for the additional cooking that happens when the bird rests before carving. Protect your arms and hands: wear those great long kitchen mitts whenever reaching into the oven. And don't use a plastic basting bulb. A soupspoon is safer for basting in this case. For one thing, the spoon is in no danger of melting.

I'm not a fan of trussing chickens. First, trussing discourages good browning and crispness. Second, today's birds are bred so that the breast and leg are finished cooking at the same time. Third, it's a pain to untruss when you are ready to serve. Roast chicken is the cornerstone of the basic recipes, but it holds its own against any complicated, expensive dish. It's a universal standard.

1	3½- to 4-pound free-range, corn-fed, or naturally raised chicken	8	medium Yellow Finn potatoes
	Kosher salt and freshly ground black pepper	8	garlic cloves
¼	cup olive oil, plus more for the chicken	8	tablespoons (1 stick) unsalted butter, at room temperature
		2	6-ounce bags spinach (or ¾ pound bulk spinach)

Heat the oven to 475 degrees.

Remove the gizzards and any extraneous fat from the chicken. Rinse and pat it dry. Salt and pepper the outside and inside well and rub the chicken with olive oil. Place the bird in a large roasting pan and roast, basting every 5 minutes with the pan juices, for 35 to 40 minutes (about 10 minutes per pound), or until an instant-read thermometer inserted in the thickest part of the thigh registers 165 degrees.

Meanwhile, scrub the potatoes (do not peel) and cut into pieces. Place in a large saucepan of cold water, add 6 of the garlic cloves and salt to taste, and bring to a boil. Reduce the heat and simmer for 25 minutes, or until the potatoes are tender. Drain, reserving ½ cup of the cooking water. Return the potatoes and garlic to the pot. Add 6 tablespoons of the butter, the ¼ cup olive oil, and the reserved potato cooking water. Mash well, using a potato masher. Taste and season with pepper, adding more salt if needed. Cover and keep warm.

Wash the spinach and cut off any large stems. Heat the remaining 2 tablespoons butter in a large skillet over medium-low heat. Add the remaining 2 garlic cloves and cook until lightly browned, about 2 minutes. Discard the garlic, add the spinach to the skillet, and cook, stirring, for 1 to 2 minutes, or until wilted. Add a good amount of salt and pepper, turn off the heat, and cover to keep warm.

When the chicken is done, remove it from the oven and let it rest for 10 minutes.

Reheat the potatoes and spinach over low heat if necessary. Carve the chicken and serve with the potatoes and spinach.

BBQ CHICKEN AND GRILLED ASPARAGUS

4 servings

My cooking career has often required quick thinking and improvisation. Before Jams opened in New York, I had committed to cooking a Citymeals-on-Wheels benefit event to be held at Jams on Friday and Saturday nights. Although construction on the restaurant was well under way, there was no banister on the staircase, no art on the walls, and no chairs. But those were the small problems—there was also no cooking equipment. I brought in two Weber grills, set them up under my exhaust hood (which didn't work), and cooked an elegant meal for sixty. This inauspicious opening must have intrigued diners enough to make them want to come back.

Since that night, I've discovered a number of tricks for grilling a chicken in a relaxed fashion. First, you can place the chicken skin side down and leave it that way for the entire grilling time with no worry of it burning or cooking unevenly. Second, you can vary the heat and cooking time, as well as the amount of smoky flavor, as necessary. And, by positioning the chicken properly, you can place all the vegetables alongside the bird, turn them only once, and they, too, will be perfectly cooked.

This backyard grilling recipe is even easy enough that you can enjoy cocktails while you cook.

1	3½- to 4¼-pound free-range, corn-fed, or naturally raised chicken
	Kosher salt and freshly ground black pepper
1	pound green beans
¼	cup extra-virgin olive oil
2	pounds thick asparagus

2	pounds new potatoes or other small potatoes (make sure they are large enough not to slip through the grilling rack)
1	tablespoon red wine vinegar
2–3	cups torn frisée lettuce
4	tablespoons (½ stick) unsalted butter, at room temperature

Prepare a hot fire in a kettle grill, such as a Weber, or heat a gas grill.

Remove the giblets and any excess fat from the chicken. Rinse and pat it dry. Butterfly the chicken by cutting down both sides of the backbone with poultry shears or sharp heavy scissors and removing the backbone (freeze it to use for stock). Open out the bird, place it skin side up on the cutting board, and press down firmly with the palms of your hands to flatten the bird as much as you can. Pat dry again. Rub the chicken lightly with salt and pepper.

Bring a large pot of salted water to a boil for the beans. Top but do not tail the beans. Cook them in the boiling water for 4 to 5 minutes, until they are just crisp-tender. Place them in a bowl and toss with 1 tablespoon of the olive oil.

Meanwhile, snap off the tough parts of the asparagus stalks. Set the asparagus aside. Scrub the potatoes.

When the grill is ready, place the chicken skin side down on the grid. Arrange the potatoes around the chicken and the asparagus off to the side, not over the coals. Immediately cover the grill! (This is extremely important—otherwise you will burn the chicken.) You will need to check every couple of minutes to ensure that the fire does not flare up. Open the vent holes in the lid three quarters of the way. Let the chicken and vegetables cook for 12 minutes, by which point the coals will have quieted down.

Turn the asparagus (not the chicken), and cook for 10 more minutes.

Remove the asparagus and turn the potatoes. After 20 more minutes, check the doneness of the potatoes and chicken (do not turn it). An instant-read thermometer inserted in the thickest part of the thigh should register 165 degrees.

Meanwhile, in a small bowl, mix together the remaining 3 tablespoons oil and the vinegar. Season well with salt and pepper. Toss the beans and frisée with the vinaigrette.

When everything is cooked, transfer the chicken to a large platter. Place the asparagus in a large bowl with the butter, toss well, and season with salt and pepper. Arrange the frisée, the potatoes, and the asparagus alongside the chicken and serve.

TURKEY BREAST MILANESE

4 servings

This dish is based on the classic veal Milanese, pounded veal scallops that are tossed in beaten eggs, breaded with fresh crumbs, and fried in butter until crisp. The technique lends itself perfectly to turkey breast fillets. This is a satisfying recipe, one that can be prepared in just a few minutes. It also works well with flatfish fillets, such as turbot and sole, as well as pounded cuts of meat, especially boneless pork loin chops.

You can prepare and fry up the turkey in the morning, refrigerate it until you're ready to serve, and reheat it in the oven for 5 minutes.

Accompany—or, more traditionally, top—the turkey with a lemony salad of mesclun, sliced cherry tomatoes, torn basil leaves, Parmesan shavings, capers, and green olives.

1 3-pound bone-in or 2-pound boneless turkey breast, free-range if possible	2 lemons
	1 pint cherry tomatoes
	20 fresh basil leaves
3 large eggs	4 tablespoons (½ stick) unsalted butter
Kosher salt	3 cups mesclun
7 tablespoons olive oil	2 tablespoons capers, rinsed and drained well
1 cup all-purpose flour	
Freshly ground black pepper	¼ cup chopped green olives
1 1-pound loaf country bread	1 tablespoon red wine vinegar

Remove the skin from the turkey. Using a sharp knife, slice the turkey diagonally into 4 equal fillets, as though you were slicing a steak.

One at a time, place each fillet between two sheets of plastic wrap and pound with a mallet until about ¼ inch thick.

In a large shallow bowl, beat the eggs with 1 teaspoon salt and 1 tablespoon of the olive oil.

Place the flour in another large shallow bowl and season with salt and pepper.

One at a time, place each fillet in the flour, dusting it well, then place in the egg mixture. Transfer to a platter and let the fillets stand for 1 hour, refrigerated.

Meanwhile, remove the crust from the bread and cut it into 1-inch cubes. Put the bread in a food processor and process to fine crumbs. Place the crumbs in a 2-quart zipper-lock plastic bag or a paper bag.

Juice the lemons; set the juice aside. Halve the cherry tomatoes. Tear the basil leaves in half.

Transfer 1 fillet to the bag with the bread crumbs, close the bag, and shake well to coat the fillet thoroughly. Place on a clean platter and repeat with the remaining 3 fillets.

Place a large skillet over medium heat and add 2 tablespoons of the olive oil and 2 tablespoons of the butter. When the mixture is golden brown, add as many of the fillets as will fit in a single layer and cook for 4 to 5 minutes, until golden brown on the first side. Gently turn over each fillet. Cook for 3 more minutes, or until cooked through. Fry the remaining fillets, using 1 more tablespoon olive oil and 1 more tablespoon butter.

Meanwhile, in a medium bowl, toss together the mesclun, tomatoes, basil, capers, and olives. Make a simple vinaigrette by whisking together the remaining 3 tablespoons olive oil, the vinegar, and salt to taste in a small bowl.

When the turkey is cooked, transfer the fillets to a platter. Wipe out the skillet with a paper towel. Melt the remaining 1 tablespoon butter in the skillet. Add the lemon juice and heat, stirring. Pour the lemon-butter mixture over the fillets.

Toss the salad with the vinaigrette and serve it beside or on top of each fillet.

SESAME GRILLED (OR BROILED) QUAIL
WITH SHOESTRING POTATOES

4 servings

Marinating the quail in a mixture of mustard, balsamic vinegar, sesame oil, and wine before cooking keeps them moist, helps crisp their skin, and gives them a rich, deep color. A final coating of toasted sesame seeds adds panache. The quail are accompanied by crispy shoestring potatoes.

The quail need to marinate for at least 2 hours, so plan accordingly. They are available through specialty butchers or through D'Artagnan (www.dartagnan.com or 800-327-8246).

1 tablespoon Dijon mustard	1 cup sesame seeds
½ cup balsamic vinegar	Kosher salt and freshly ground
1 teaspoon toasted sesame oil	black pepper
¼ cup dry white wine	About 4 cups corn oil or peanut oil,
1 tablespoon olive oil	for deep-frying
1 garlic clove	24 fresh basil leaves
1 shallot	24 fresh sage leaves
8 quail (see above)	24 large fresh flat-leaf parsley leaves
3 russet potatoes (about 2½ pounds total)	(optional)

Whisk the mustard, vinegar, and sesame oil in a small bowl. Whisk in the wine, then dribble in the olive oil, whisking until the mixture emulsifies. Finely mince the garlic and shallot and stir them into the marinade. Let sit for 30 minutes at room temperature.

Meanwhile, rinse the birds in cold water and pat them dry. Butterfly each quail by cutting down both sides of the backbone with poultry shears or sharp heavy scissors and removing it (freeze the backbones to use for stock, if you like). Open out each bird and place skin side up on the cutting board. Press down firmly with the palms of your hands to flatten the birds as much as you can. Pat dry again.

Strain the marinade into a shallow dish large enough to hold all the quail in a single layer. Place them skin side down in the marinade, cover, and refrigerate for 1 hour. Turn the quail, cover, and refrigerate for at least 1 hour longer, or up to overnight.

Peel the potatoes. With a mandoline or sharp knife, cut them into matchsticks. As you work, immediately place the potatoes in a bowl of ice water; then refrigerate. The potatoes must be kept absolutely ice cold.

Prepare a medium fire in a grill or heat the broiler.

Place the sesame seeds in a small dry skillet and toast over low heat, flipping the skillet every 10 seconds, until the seeds are golden. Pour the seeds onto a plate to cool.

Transfer the quail to a platter, reserving the marinade. Do not dry the quail. Season lightly with salt and pepper and set aside. Bring the marinade to a boil in a small saucepan; set aside.

TO FRY THE POTATOES

Pour the corn or peanut oil into a large heavy pot and heat the oil to 370 degrees. Remove the potatoes from the ice water and spin-dry in a salad spinner, then pat them dry with a large kitchen towel—they must be absolutely dry. Place a few of the potato sticks in the oil to check the temperature; if they color too quickly, lower the heat slightly. Being careful to avoid splattering, lower the potatoes into the oil with a wire frying basket or Chinese mesh strainer. Push the potatoes around a bit so they don't stick together. When just golden, after about 6 minutes, remove them and place them in a bowl lined with paper towels. Salt lightly.

Pat the herbs thoroughly dry, add to the hot oil, and fry for about 1 minute, until crisp and jade green. Remove with a slotted spoon and drain on paper towels.

TO GRILL THE QUAIL

Place the quail skin side down over the fire and grill until mahogany colored, about 3 minutes. Turn the quail and grill until just cooked through, about 7 minutes longer, basting with the reserved marinade once or twice.

TO BROIL THE QUAIL

Place the quail skin side up on the broiler pan and broil for 2 to 3 minutes, until mahogany colored. Turn and broil, basting once or twice with the marinade, until just cooked through, 2 to 3 minutes longer.

When the quail are done, press the skin side of each one into the toasted sesame seeds to coat. Place on a platter and cover loosely with foil in a warm oven.

Quickly divide the shoestring potatoes into 4 parts and arrange on serving plates, forming each into a nest large enough to hold 2 quail. Arrange 2 quail in each nest, scatter the fried herb leaves over them, and serve at once.

SQUAB AND CORN CREPES

4 servings

This spicy, sensuous, elegant dish propels crepes into another dimension. The crepes, made from a chunky batter of potato, chile, and corn, are topped with pan-fried squab and sauced with a corn-and-chive sauce made from a simple squab stock. The result is at once rustic and sophisticated.

Squab are available from specialty butchers or D'Artagnan (www.dartagnan .com or 800-327-8246).

4	squab (see above)		Kosher salt and freshly ground
1	medium red onion		black pepper
4	garlic cloves, not peeled	1	cup milk
½	cup dry white wine	3	large eggs
1	bouquet garni (see page 5)	¼	cup all-purpose flour
1	poblano chile	2	tablespoons olive oil
1	large russet potato	½	cup chopped fresh chives
3	ears corn	1	lime
	About 8 tablespoons (1 stick)		
	unsalted butter		

Heat the oven to 350 degrees.

Butterfly each squab by cutting down both sides of the backbone with poultry shears or sharp heavy scissors and removing the backbone; reserve the backbones. Open out the birds and place skin side up on the cutting board. Press down firmly with the palms of your hands to flatten the birds as much as you can. Place the squab on a platter, cover, and refrigerate.

MAKE THE STOCK

Slice the onion. Place the squab bones in a small roasting pan with the onion and unpeeled garlic cloves and roast for 25 minutes, turning the bones and vegetables every 10 minutes.

Remove the pan from the oven and transfer the bones and vegetables to a large saucepan. Discard the fat in the roasting pan and deglaze the pan with the wine, then pour into the saucepan. Cover the bones with water, toss in the bouquet garni, and simmer, skimming off the foam as necessary, for 1½ hours, or until flavorful. Strain the stock and set aside.

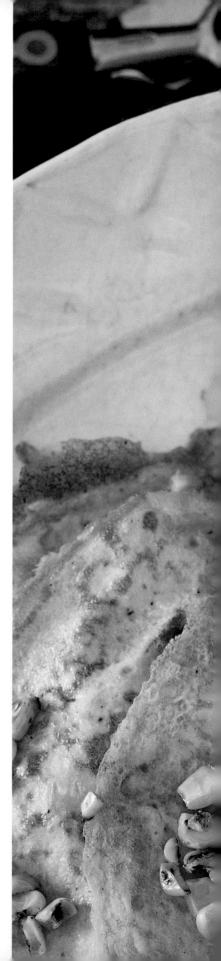

MAKE THE CREPE BATTER

Mince the chile finely. Peel and cut the potato into a small dice. Place the potato in a small saucepan of cold water, bring the water to a boil, and cook until the potato is al dente, about 10 minutes; drain.

Husk the corn, cut the kernels off the corncobs, and place them in a bowl.

Melt 2 tablespoons of the butter in a large skillet. Add half the corn and sauté until tender. Salt and pepper lightly, transfer the cooked corn to a small bowl, and let cool.

Stir the milk into the cooked corn. Crack the eggs into a large bowl; add the flour and mix well. Stir in the chile, the potato, and the corn mixture. Melt 3 tablespoons of the butter and add to the crepe batter; it will be as thin as pancake batter. Season to taste with salt and pepper and set aside.

COOK THE CREPES

Heat a well-seasoned crepe pan or skillet over medium heat. Melt 1 tablespoon of the remaining butter in the pan, then add about ¼ cup batter and tilt the pan to spread the batter. Cook, turning once, until golden brown on each side. (The crepes may be a little difficult to flip because of their chunky texture.) Fold the crepe in half or into quarters and place on a plate. Repeat, making 4 crepes in all, using about 1 tablespoon butter for each batch as needed.

COOK THE SQUAB

Salt and pepper both sides of the squab. Heat 1 tablespoon of the olive oil in the skillet over medium heat (use two skillets to speed up the

process, if you like). Add 2 of the squab, skin side down, and cook for 10 minutes. Turn the squab and cook until rare, about 130 degrees. Transfer the squab to a platter and cover to keep warm. Cook the remaining squab, using the remaining 1 tablespoon olive oil, and remove from the pan.

Add the rest of the corn to the pan and sauté for 2 minutes, stirring constantly. Add 1½ cups of the stock and simmer for 5 minutes. Turn off the heat and cover to keep warm. Reserve the rest of the stock for another use.

To finish the squab, heat the broiler. Place the squab skin side up on a rack in the broiler pan and broil until the skin crackles and the thighs register about 140 degrees. Let stand for 5 minutes; the final temperature should be about 145 degrees (medium-rare).

Meanwhile, reheat the sauce and stir in the chives. Cut the lime into wedges.

Arrange the crepes on serving plates and put a squab on top of each crepe. Spoon the sauce on top of each squab and decorate the plates with wedges of lime.

PHEASANT WITH OYSTER STUFFING

4 or 8 servings

Pheasants are now plentiful in many markets, thanks to certain poultry farmers who discovered that money was to be made by selling them at $5 a pound—a little more profitable than chickens, which generally sell for a mere 80 cents per pound!

This recipe is complex, but if you divide the steps into three parts, first making the stuffing, then cooking the birds in a red wine bath, and finally finishing the sauce and carving the pheasant, it's not too difficult. Braising the birds in a good Cabernet Sauvignon keeps them moist and turns them a lovely reddish hue. The resulting sauce is memorable. The oysters for the stuffing must be fresh, large, and briny, and the sourdough bread should be quite tangy.

1	sourdough baguette
1	garlic head, plus 2 cloves
14	tablespoons (1¾ sticks) unsalted butter
2	ears corn
	Kosher salt and freshly ground black pepper
12	shucked oysters, with their juices
1	cup julienned Smithfield ham, serrano ham, or prosciutto
4	fresh oregano sprigs

3	fresh sage sprigs
3	fresh tarragon sprigs
1	medium head radicchio
2	3-pound pheasants
2	medium onions
1	750-ml bottle Cabernet Sauvignon
1	bouquet garni (see page 5; include the stems from the oregano, sage, and tarragon)

Cut the baguette into 1-inch cubes. Smash the 2 garlic cloves. Melt 4 tablespoons of the butter in a large skillet over medium heat. Add the smashed garlic and the croutons and sauté the croutons until they're deep golden brown, 5 to 8 minutes. Transfer them to a large bowl. Discard the garlic.

Husk the corn and cut the kernels off the corncobs with a sharp knife. Melt 2 tablespoons of the butter in a medium skillet and sauté the

corn until tender. Salt and pepper the corn judiciously and add it to the croutons.

Coarsely chop the oysters and add them, along with their juices, to the croutons. Add the ham and toss to mix.

Remove the herb leaves, saving the stems for the bouquet garni, and chop the leaves. Julienne the radicchio. Add the herbs and radicchio to the stuffing and mix well. Melt 2 tablespoons

of the butter and add to the bowl, mixing well. Taste for salt and pepper, remembering that the oysters and ham are salty.

Place half of the stuffing into the cavity of each pheasant. Sew up the cavities with butcher's twine, then sew the neck cavities shut so the birds are fairly watertight.

Heat the oven to 375 degrees.

Cut the onions into ½-inch cubes. Cut the head of garlic horizontally in half. Set aside.

Melt 4 tablespoons of the butter over medium heat in a lidded enameled cast-iron casserole or Dutch oven large enough to hold the 2 pheasants side by side. Salt and pepper the pheasants and brown each bird lightly on all sides, 3 to 4 minutes per side. Pour the Cabernet Sauvignon into the casserole. Add the onions, garlic, and bouquet garni and bring the mixture to a boil.

Cover the casserole tightly and transfer to the oven. You'll need to baste the pheasants every 10 minutes with the cooking liquid. They will take approximately 10 minutes per pound, or about 30 minutes total; when they are done, the legs will just begin to pull away from the body.

With tongs or a large slotted spoon, transfer the pheasants to a platter; cover them loosely to keep warm. Carefully strain the cooking liquid through a cheesecloth-lined sieve into a saucepan; discard the solids. Bring to a boil and reduce the liquid to 3 cups.

Cut away the twine from the birds and scoop out the stuffing, dividing it among four or eight plates. Carve the pheasants and give each person half a breast and half a leg, or half a pheasant each if you're feeding four hungry people. Swirl the remaining 2 tablespoons of butter into the sauce, spoon the sauce over the pheasant, and serve.

A GOOD BUTCHER
IS A TREASURE.
MAKE HIM HAPPY!
HE HAS EVERYTHING
TO GAIN FROM YOU
KNOWING MEAT WELL.

MEAT AND

GAME

Meat is best at your local butcher shop. A good butcher is a treasure. Make him happy! He has a lot of competition, and he has everything to gain from you knowing meat well. He will go out of his way to select well-marbled meat for you. So don't be shy around him. Ask him if the skirt steak is better than the flank today. Don't hesitate to return to him with your comments—he's not thin-skinned. He'll tell you when the filets mignons are at their cheapest—and at their best.

Go for free-range, grass-fed animals, which are the tastiest and the most humanely treated.

Pork has made a well-deserved comeback in the past few years, because of its versatility, taste, and cost. The new respect has been a boon to the pork industry. Unfortunately, good pork is difficult to find. Tell your butcher that you want local pigs that are not lean. For some unfathomable reason, the pork industry began raising lean pigs. How silly—a fat pig is a good pig! We are lucky indeed to have a small cottage industry of farmers who have dedicated themselves to bringing back real pigs. These ranchers come from every part of the United States. Their products are more expensive, but they are well worth the price.

When I was growing up, my family raised gorgeous lamb on our little farm. We ate fall lamb (50 pounds), yearling lamb (85 pounds dressed), true spring lamb (between 20 and 30 pounds), and mutton.

Your butcher can provide you with domestic, New Zealand, or Australian lamb. If you're lucky enough to know a local farmer who raises lamb, don't hesitate to order a whole one and have it butchered. Shoulders and legs do quite well in the freezer, but ribs and saddle should be cooked fresh. Lamb liver, sweetbreads, and kidneys are also wonderful.

Domestic lambs yield a heavy chop or rack and large legs that will feed up to eight people. New Zealand lambs are spring lambs, with tiny chops and legs. Australian lambs are bigger and meatier, right in between the tiny New Zealand lambs and the large domestic. Which is the best? They all serve their purposes. I love a good saddle of domestic grass-fed lamb that, depending on the season, can be sweet or slightly gamy. True New Zealand spring lamb is almost entirely milk-fed with just a bit of grazing, which results in a grayish-pink meat that cooks up sweet and meltingly tender. Australian lamb is great for barbecuing or for formal crown roasts or whole saddles. But I think the best lambs of all are Sonoma lambs. These beauties are as close to those mythical milk-fed Brittany lambs as you will see. Sonoma lambs are difficult to find and expensive (excellent lambs are available by mail-order from Niman Ranch), but worth every penny. They can be roasted whole, and each cut is as tender and flavorful as the next.

For humanely raised, flavorful veal, look for meat labeled "grass-fed," "free-range," or "certified organic." These yearlings are humanely raised and fed for three months on mother's milk, not formula.

Farm-raised venison is a flavorful and lean change of pace from beef. It's available fresh or frozen from a number of Internet sources. I prefer domestic venison, but Australian and New Zealand venison is quite good.

Rabbit is a succulent and versatile meat. Sauces made from rabbit bones are delicate, refined, and utterly delicious. Use only fresh rabbit. Size is important: if they're too small, there won't be enough meat. Few dishes are as satisfying as the grilled rabbit recipe I've included here.

MEAT AND GAME

STEAK TARTARE WITH MELTED RACLETTE AND POTATOES

4 servings

On a New Year's holiday skiing trip in Zermatt, Switzerland, I fell instantly in love with a dish of roasted new potatoes served with a melted coating of raclette cheese. The nutty mountain cheese was a perfect foil for the potatoes. I decided they would be just the thing to serve with steak tartare. The tartare is surrounded by accompaniments—chiles, parsley, onion—so everyone can mix their own and make the tartare as spicy as they wish.

1 pound filet mignon or boneless rib-eye steak	1 Meyer lemon or regular lemon
2 pounds new potatoes or small red potatoes	1 jalapeño chile
1 tablespoon extra-virgin olive oil	1 serrano chile
Sea salt and freshly ground black pepper	½ red onion
3 shallots	¼ cup fresh flat-leaf parsley leaves
4 garlic cloves	1 large tomato
	1 lime
	½ pound raclette cheese
	Tabasco sauce

Trim any fat from the meat. With a sharp knife, slice the beef as thin as possible, removing any sinew. Stack the slices and slice them into ⅛-inch-wide strips, then cut the strips into a small dice. Cover and refrigerate.

Put the potatoes in a large saucepan of salted cold water over high heat. Boil the potatoes in their skins until tender but still firm, 12 to 20 minutes. Drain and let cool, then thinly slice. Place in a medium bowl and toss with the olive oil. Season with salt and pepper.

Meanwhile, mince the shallots and garlic. Juice the lemon. Mince the chiles, onion, and parsley. Core and finely chop the tomato. Cut the lime into wedges. Grate the cheese; set aside.

To finish the tartare, mix the meat with a good amount of salt and pepper. Add the shallots and garlic and mix well. Add the lemon juice to the meat along with a few shakes of Tabasco sauce and mix well. Divide the mixture into 4 portions and mound the meat on four plates. Spoon a little of the minced chiles, onion, parsley, and tomato around each mound and place a wedge or two of lime on each plate.

Heat the broiler. Spread the potatoes on a baking sheet and crisp them under the broiler for a few minutes, until they start to brown. Spread the cheese over the potatoes and return the sheet to the broiler for 2 to 3 minutes to melt the cheese. When it is bubbly, divide the potatoes among the plates and serve at once.

FILET MIGNON WITH PEPPER-POTATO GRATIN

8 servings

Seasoning the steak with a spice rub of four types of peppercorns—pink, black, white, and green—gives it complexity; orange zest creates exotic undertones. The orange sauce is slightly tropical and fresh-tasting, not sweet.

The gratin is a spicy, lusty version of the creamy potato gratin served in the Beaujolais region of France, with the addition of roasted bell peppers and poblano chiles and garlic.

2 tablespoons black peppercorns
2 tablespoons white peppercorns
2 tablespoons pink peppercorns
2 tablespoons green peppercorns
2 oranges
2 tablespoons kosher salt
4 pounds filet mignon

Gratin
2 pounds russet potatoes
2 red bell peppers
2 yellow bell peppers
2 green bell peppers

6 poblano chiles
3 garlic cloves
1 cup milk
    Kosher salt and freshly ground
        black pepper
4 tablespoons (½ stick) unsalted butter,
        plus more for the baking dish
1 cup heavy cream
1 small cinnamon stick

    Olive oil, for the steaks
4 tablespoons (½ stick) unsalted butter

MAKE THE SPICE RUB

Heat the oven to 350 degrees.

Spread the peppercorns on a baking sheet and toast in the oven for 5 minutes. Coarsely grind them in a spice mill or coffee grinder.

Grate the zest from the oranges. Mix it with the peppercorns and salt and spread out on a plate to dry. Juice the oranges and reserve the juice.

Trim the beef of fat and sinew (I like to leave on a little fat to crisp and to give a little moisture to the meat). Cut into 8 steaks of equal thickness. Set aside.

MAKE THE GRATIN

Peel the potatoes and place them in cold water. Roast the bell peppers and chiles over medium-high heat on the stovetop or under a hot broiler, turning occasionally, until blackened and blistered all over. Place them in a bowl, cover with plastic wrap, and let steam for 15 minutes.

Peel the peppers and chiles with your fingers (do not rinse) and stem and seed them. Cut them in half, keeping the peppers and chiles separate.

Heat the oven to 375 degrees. Butter an 8-x-10 or similar-size Pyrex baking dish or earthenware casserole and rub the inside with one of the garlic cloves.

Put the milk and the garlic cloves in a medium saucepan and bring to a boil over medium heat, then reduce the heat and simmer for 10 minutes to infuse the flavor. Remove the garlic from the milk and discard the garlic. Keep the milk warm.

Drain the potatoes. Using a mandoline or sharp knife, slice the potatoes wafer-thin. Make a layer of about one third of the potatoes in the baking dish. Season with salt and pepper, and add a layer of all the halved poblano chiles. Dot with butter and pour in one third of the milk. Add another one third of the potatoes, salt and pepper them, and add a layer of all the halved bell peppers. Dot with butter, add another third of the milk, add the remaining potatoes, and sprinkle with salt and pepper. Dot with the rest of the butter and pour the remaining milk over the top.

Place the gratin in the oven and bake for 20 minutes, or until the milk has been absorbed by the potatoes.

Heat the cream with the cinnamon stick in a medium saucepan over medium heat until it is hot. Keep warm over low heat.

Remove and discard the cinnamon stick and pour the cream into the gratin. Bake the gratin for another 20 minutes, until the potatoes are tender and the top is golden brown and slightly crispy. Remove the gratin from the oven and set aside in a warm place.

COOK THE STEAKS

Meanwhile, if you are going to grill the steaks, prepare a hot fire in a grill.

Brush each steak with olive oil, then dip in the peppercorn-zest mixture, turning to coat.

TO GRILL THE STEAKS

Grill the steaks, turning once, until they're crusty on the outside but still rare inside, about 5 minutes on each side.

TO PANFRY THE STEAKS

Heat 2 tablespoons olive oil in a large cast-iron skillet over high heat for 5 minutes (or use two large skillets if you have them). Add 2 steaks, reduce the heat to medium-high, and cook, turning once, for about 5 minutes per side for rare. Transfer to a platter and cover to keep warm while you cook the rest of the steaks.

Let the steaks rest while you make the sauce. Melt the butter in a small saucepan and cook until golden brown. Carefully pour in the reserved orange juice and cook, stirring occasionally, for a few minutes, until reduced and thickened.

Place the steaks on eight plates and top with the sauce. Serve a generous helping of gratin alongside each steak.

SKIRT OR HANGER STEAK MARINATED IN SOY, GINGER, AND LIME WITH RED ONION TOASTS

4 servings

This recipe is my take on fast food. Skirt steak comes from the flank, or diaphragm, of the cow. It was sold cheaply for years because few people were aware of its tenderness and deep flavor. Now, thanks to the ubiquity of fajitas, which popularized this cut, skirt steak has become pricier, but it has no surface fat or bone, so nothing is wasted. Because it's so thin, the steak can be on the table in less than 10 minutes.

The marinade brings out the assertive beefy flavors.

2 pounds skirt or hanger steak	3 shallots
1 2-inch piece fresh ginger	2 tablespoons unsalted butter
1 lime	Kosher salt and freshly ground
¼ cup soy sauce	black pepper
3 garlic cloves	1 red onion
1 cup dry red wine	4 slices sourdough bread

Pat the steak dry with paper towels and place it in a nonreactive baking pan.

Peel and grate the ginger. Juice the lime. In a small bowl, mix the ginger with the lime juice and soy sauce. Smash 2 of the garlic cloves and add them to the marinade. Pour the mixture over the steak, cover, and marinate in the refrigerator for 2 hours.

Remove the steak from the marinade and place on a platter. Discard the garlic and ginger and reserve the marinade.

Bring the red wine to a boil in a small saucepan over medium-high heat. Chop the shallots and add them to the wine. Boil to reduce the wine to

¼ cup. Stir in the butter and salt and pepper to taste. Set aside.

Meanwhile, heat the broiler. Slice the onion into ¼-inch-thick rounds and place on a baking sheet. Sprinkle with the reserved marinade and broil the onion until tender and dark brown, about 10 minutes; be careful not to burn it. Transfer to a plate and set aside. Leave the broiler on.

Place the steak on the broiler pan and broil, turning once, just until medium-rare, about 4 minutes per side. Transfer to a cutting board and cover loosely to keep warm.

Toast the bread on both sides under the broiler.

Meanwhile, reheat the sauce over low heat.

Split the remaining garlic clove in half and rub the slices of toast with the garlic. Place a slice of toast on each plate. Divide the onion among the toasts. Slice the steak and place on the plates. Top the steak with the red wine sauce and serve.

BRINED PORK LOIN
WITH HUCKLEBERRIES OR BLUEBERRIES

8 to 10 servings

Pork takes to brining better than any other meat. Brining tenderizes the meat and amplifies its flavor and richness. After the brining has worked its magic (you'll need to brine the pork overnight), the meat is ready to be braised.

The season for huckleberries is usually late summer into autumn, but they can arrive as early as July or even as late as January, depending on the quixotic weather of the Northwest. Huckleberries resemble small blueberries, but they have noticeable seeds and are tarter. Blueberries can be substituted. Beaujolais adds an acidic fruitiness that brings the sauce and pork together.

1	4-pound boneless center-cut pork loin roast	1	celery stalk
	Kosher salt	½	pound (2 sticks) unsalted butter, at room temperature
¼	cup sugar	2	bay leaves
8	carrots	2	cups Beaujolais Nouveau or Zinfandel
2	large onions	2	pounds new potatoes or other small potatoes
15	garlic cloves		Freshly ground black pepper
9	shallots	2	pints huckleberries or blueberries
1	2-inch piece fresh ginger	¼	cup red wine vinegar
2	large leeks		

Trim the pork loin of excess fat and sinew (I like to leave a ¼-inch layer of fat to keep the roast moist). In a small saucepan, combine ¼ cup kosher salt, the sugar, and 2 cups water and bring to a boil, stirring to dissolve the salt and sugar. Remove from the heat and let cool.

Place the pork in a large bowl and pour the brine over it. Cover the pork and refrigerate overnight, turning it twice.

Heat the oven to 325 degrees.

Peel the carrots, onions, garlic cloves, shallots, and ginger. Trim the leeks and wash them well. Cut the carrots, leeks, and celery into 3-inch lengths; quarter the onions.

Remove the pork from the brine and rinse and dry it thoroughly. Melt 1 stick of the butter in an enameled cast-iron casserole or Dutch oven over medium-high heat. Add the pork (no salt and pepper) and brown it on all sides, about 10 minutes. Transfer to a plate and set aside.

Add the carrots, onions, shallots, ginger, and garlic to the casserole and brown them all over. Add the leeks, celery, and bay leaves, then add the pork, wine, and enough water to cover the pork. Bring the liquid to a boil and cover the pot.

Transfer the casserole to the oven and cook for 30 to 45 minutes, or until the meat is fork-tender.

Remove the casserole from the oven, transfer the pork to a platter, and set aside, loosely covered. Boil the cooking liquid over medium-high heat to reduce it to 2 cups. Strain the liquid, discarding the vegetables, and clean out the pot. Return the pork and the reduced braising liquid to the pot and cover to keep warm.

Meanwhile, peel the potatoes and cut them into small chunks. Place them in a large saucepan, cover them with cold water, and add salt to taste. Bring to a boil, then reduce the heat and simmer until the potatoes are tender, 10 to 15 minutes. Drain the potatoes, return them to the saucepan, and mash them with a potato masher. Stir in the remaining stick of butter and salt and pepper to taste. Keep warm.

Rinse and pick over the huckleberries or blueberries. Put the vinegar in a medium saucepan, add a few of the berries, and smash them. Bring to a boil over medium-high heat and cook until lightly thickened. Transfer the pork to a carving board. Add the reduced braising liquid and the remaining berries to the vinegar mixture. Bring to a simmer and simmer for 2 minutes.

Slice the pork into thin slices and arrange on a platter. Pour the berry sauce over the pork and serve with the mashed potatoes.

PORK TENDERLOIN
WITH PORTOBELLO MUSHROOM SAUCE

4 servings

Pork tenderloin, the muscle located underneath the loin and ribs, was largely ignored until about the mid-1980s, when chefs of my generation began cooking them in unusual and interesting ways. The public caught on. Unfortunately, so did the butchers—and the price of pork tenderloin doubled. The good news is that this most delicious of all pork cuts has very little waste. The tenderloin is hard to cook badly—unlike pork chops, which can become tough and dry—and easy to cook well. It should be cooked to medium (pink), not well-done, so it stays moist.

2 pounds pork tenderloin (2–3 tenderloins)	2 fennel bulbs
1 small onion	½ pound portobello mushrooms
1 garlic clove	3 shallots
A handful of fresh parsley stems	6 tablespoons olive oil
1 cup Merlot	10 tablespoons (1 stick plus 2 tablespoons) unsalted butter
4 new potatoes or other small potatoes	Kosher salt and freshly ground black pepper
2 medium parsnips	1 cup chicken broth or veal broth
2 medium turnips	
1 rutabaga	

Remove any silverskin (tough sinew) from the pork. Slice the onion and put it in a large bowl. Smash the garlic. Add the garlic, parsley stems, and Merlot to the bowl and stir well. Add the pork, turning it in the marinade. Cover and marinate, refrigerated, for 1 to 2 hours, turning the pork occasionally.

Heat the oven to 450 degrees.

Peel the potatoes, parsnips, turnips, and rutabaga and cut them into bite-sized pieces.

Put them in a bowl of cold water. Trim the fennel, cut lengthwise in half, and remove the cores.

Stem the mushrooms and place them gill side up on a baking sheet. Mince the shallots and mix with 2 tablespoons of the olive oil. Spoon the shallot mixture onto the mushroom caps.

Roast the mushrooms for 5 to 8 minutes, or until hot, so they absorb the flavors of the shallots. Remove the mushrooms, dice them, and transfer to a medium saucepan. (Leave the oven on.)

Melt 6 tablespoons of the butter in a small saucepan. Drain the root vegetables and put them and the fennel in a large bowl. Toss with the melted butter, 2 tablespoons of the olive oil, and salt and pepper to taste. Transfer to a large baking pan, add ½ cup water, and roast for 40 minutes, turning the vegetables occasionally.

Meanwhile, remove the pork from the marinade and strain the marinade into the saucepan with the mushrooms. Add the broth, bring to a simmer on low heat, and simmer for 20 minutes, until slightly thickened. Remove from the heat.

Pat the pork dry with paper towels. Salt and pepper it, brush it with the remaining 2 tablespoons oil, and place on a small rimmed baking sheet. When the vegetables have roasted for 10 minutes, place the pork in the oven and roast for 20 minutes, turning once, or until an instant-read thermometer registers 145 degrees. Transfer the pork to a carving board and let rest for 10 minutes.

While the pork rests, bring the mushroom mixture back to a simmer. Stir in the remaining 4 tablespoons butter and season with salt and pepper to taste.

Carve the pork into ¼-inch-thick slices. Place the pork on a platter, cover with the roasted vegetables, and spoon over the portobello sauce. Serve.

PORK SHOULDER
WITH MOLE SAUCE

PORK SHOULDER
WITH MOLE SAUCE

6 to 8 servings

Mole is a piquant sauce that sounds exotic, but this stew is simple to make. It does contain three different kinds of chiles, but they are available in many large supermarkets as well as specialty produce shops. The mole is enhanced by a little unsweetened chocolate and bacon, which imparts smokiness, saltiness, and a rich creamy quality.

This cut is sometimes called Boston butt, even though it's nowhere near the posterior of the pig. The alternate name goes back to pre-Revolutionary New England, when highly valued ("high on the hog") cuts of pork were stored in barrels called butts. Note that the pork must marinate for at least 8 hours.

4	pounds boneless pork shoulder
12	garlic cloves
1	bunch fresh cilantro
2	cups sake
2	dried pasilla chiles
2	serrano chiles
1	habanero chile
2	medium onions
¼	pound thick-cut bacon
4	ripe tomatoes or drained canned plum tomatoes, preferably San Marzano
	Kosher salt
3–4	tablespoons unsalted butter

1	cup chicken broth
1	cup basmati rice
	Freshly ground black pepper

For finishing the stew

4	ounces unsweetened chocolate
2	tablespoons unsalted butter, at room temperature
¼	cup all-purpose flour

Warmed corn tortillas or corn bread, for serving

AT LEAST 8 HOURS OR THE DAY BEFORE, MARINATE THE PORK
Cut the pork into 1-inch cubes and place in a large bowl. Smash 2 of the garlic cloves. Remove the leaves from the cilantro and reserve them for garnish. Chop the cilantro stems and add them to the pork, along with the smashed garlic. Pour in the sake and stir well. Cover and refrigerate for at least 8 hours, or overnight, turning the pork occasionally.

MAKE THE STEW

Soak the pasilla chiles in warm water until soft, about an hour. Stem, seed, and finely chop them.

Meanwhile, roast the serrano and habanero chiles over medium-high heat on the stovetop or under a hot broiler, turning occasionally, until blackened and blistered all over. Place the chiles in a bowl, cover with plastic wrap, and let steam for 15 minutes.

Peel the roasted chiles with your fingers (do not rinse); stem, seed, and finely chop them. Mix all the chiles together.

Chop the onions. Mince the remaining 10 garlic cloves. Cut the bacon into 1-x-¼-inch strips. Core, seed, and chop the fresh tomatoes or seed and chop the canned tomatoes.

Place a large enameled cast-iron casserole or Dutch oven over medium heat and cook the bacon until it renders some of its fat, about 5 minutes. Add the onions, garlic, half the chiles, and the tomatoes and sauté until the onions are tender, 8 to 10 minutes. Transfer the bacon and vegetables to a bowl and set aside. Wipe out the pot.

Remove the pork from the marinade (reserving the marinade) and pat it dry with paper towels. Season it with salt and pepper. Melt 2 tablespoons of the butter in the pot and brown the pork, in batches, over medium-high heat using 1 more tablespoon butter if needed. Transfer the pork to a plate as it is browned.

Strain the marinade and deglaze the casserole with the marinade and chicken broth, stirring to scrape up the browned bits. Return the pork and bacon mixture to the casserole and bring to a boil. Reduce the heat to a quiet simmer and cook, covered, for 2 hours, or until the pork is very tender.

Meanwhile, about 20 minutes before the pork is cooked, rinse the rice three times and place it in a medium saucepan with 2 cups cold water, the remaining 1 tablespoon butter, and salt and pepper to taste. Bring the mixture to a boil, cover the pan, reduce the heat to low, and cook the rice for 20 minutes, or until it is tender. Remove from the heat and keep warm.

FINISH THE STEW

Chop the chocolate. Mix the 2 tablespoons butter with the flour in a small bowl, blending it well with your fingers, then mix in the reserved chiles. Whisk the butter mixture into the stew. Add the chocolate, increase the heat to medium, and cook, stirring, for 10 minutes.

Spoon the rice onto six to eight plates, top with the stew, and garnish with the reserved cilantro leaves. Serve with warmed tortillas or corn bread.

LAMB T-BONES AND EGGPLANT

4 servings

A lamb T-bone is like a wonderfully plump, juicy, smaller version of a beef T-bone steak, carved from the center of the loin. One glorious summer evening not long ago, Chalone Vineyards asked me to prepare a meal for their tenth anniversary at the winery, in the Pinnacle Mountains, near Monterey, California. The company rented some outdoor grills, and we cooked all the food alfresco. The hit of the evening was these T-bones, marinated in red wine (Carmenet, of course). Japanese eggplants are small, narrow, and purple. When they are cooked on the grill, they burst into a sweet, succulent, and tender mass.

The supermarket often carries lamb T-bones in packages of two or three, but if you can't find them, buy a bone-in loin of lamb and ask the butcher if he wouldn't mind buzzing it into thick chops.

1 large onion	8 fresh parsley sprigs
3 garlic cloves	2 fresh rosemary sprigs
1 cup hearty red wine, such as Zinfandel	4 Japanese eggplants or small regular eggplants
6 tablespoons olive oil	Kosher salt and freshly ground
8 lamb T-bones, 1½ inches thick (see headnote)	black pepper

Slice the onion. Smash the garlic. Put the red wine, 3 tablespoons of the olive oil, and the garlic in a bowl large enough to hold the lamb and stir. Pat the T-bones dry and place them in the marinade, turning to coat. Scatter the onion slices over the steaks. Add the parsley and the rosemary sprigs. Let the lamb marinate, covered with plastic wrap and refrigerated, for 3 hours; turn the lamb once or twice.

Prepare a medium-hot fire in a grill. Cut the eggplants lengthwise in half. Coat with the remaining 3 tablespoons olive oil and sprinkle with salt and pepper.

Grill the eggplant halves, cut side down, to seal the outside, about 3 minutes. Turn the eggplants and cook until they begin to puff, about 5 minutes. Remove from the grill and keep on a platter in a warm spot.

Pat the steaks dry and season them with salt and pepper. Grill them for about 3 minutes per side for medium-rare. Transfer the steaks to a platter and let rest for about 5 minutes.

Place a T-bone and 2 eggplant halves on each plate and serve.

BRAISED LAMB SHOULDER WITH FRIED SHALLOTS

6 to 8 servings

This American version of a French daube replaces the traditional beef with lamb. The lamb shoulder is seared briefly, then braised in wine and herbs with aromatic vegetables. It is served with its braising juices and garnished with fried shallots. Be sure to accompany it with a lusty red wine, such as the same Chianti you used for braising.

It's crucial here to choose the proper cooking vessel. I like the big terra-cotta pots from Spain that are glazed on the outside. They conduct heat very well without the risk of cracking. If such a pot isn't available to you, use an enameled cast-iron casserole, such as Le Creuset, or other Dutch oven with a good lid.

1¼ cups olive oil
   Kosher salt and freshly ground
      black pepper
1 6-pound boneless lamb
      shoulder roast
2 cups Chianti
2 large white onions
2 carrots
2 leeks

8 garlic cloves
2 jalapeño chiles
½ cup kalamata olives
1 bay leaf
1½ teaspoons fresh thyme leaves
5 drained canned plum tomatoes,
      preferably San Marzano
5 shallots
2 tablespoons all-purpose flour

Heat ¼ cup of the olive oil in a large enameled cast-iron casserole or Dutch oven over medium-high heat. Salt and pepper the lamb and sear it on all sides, giving the meat a good golden color, about 20 minutes. Transfer the lamb to a platter. Deglaze the pot with the wine, stirring up the browned bits. Return the lamb to the casserole and set aside.

Heat the oven to 325 degrees.

Cut the onions into 1-inch pieces. Peel the carrots and cut into 1-inch pieces. Wash and trim the leeks and cut them into 4-inch lengths. Halve the garlic cloves. Stem and chop the chiles. Pit and chop the olives. Add the onions, carrots, leeks, garlic, chiles, olives, bay leaf, and thyme to the casserole, scattering them around the lamb. Chop the tomatoes and add them as well. Add enough water to come up to just below the top of the lamb and bring to a simmer.

Cover the pot tightly, set in the hot oven, and cook for 4 hours, or until the lamb is very tender and falling apart. Remove the casserole from the oven and skim off the fat from the liquid. Discard the bay leaf and cover the stew to keep it hot.

Meanwhile, thinly slice the shallots.

Place the flour on a plate and toss the shallots in the flour. Heat the remaining 1 cup olive oil in a large skillet to 325 degrees. Fry the shallots, in batches if necessary, until crispy. Remove with a slotted spoon and drain on paper towels. Salt them.

Spoon a good piece of lamb (it will break apart into large chunks), a bit of braising liquid, and some vegetables into bowls. Top with the fried shallots and serve.

VEAL CHOPS WITH ROASTED PEARL ONIONS

4 servings

Chops are the quintessential American cut of meat. Easy to prepare and hefty, they entice you into picking them up and gnawing on the bone. These are served with roasted pearl onions glazed with balsamic vinegar.

6 fresh rosemary sprigs, plus more for garnish	Kosher salt and freshly ground black pepper
½ lemon	2 pounds pearl onions, unpeeled
8 tablespoons (1 stick) plus 3–6 more tablespoons unsalted butter, at room temperature	4 veal chops, 1½ inches thick
	¼ cup balsamic vinegar

Heat the oven to 425 degrees.

Pull off 1 tablespoon rosemary leaves from a couple of the sprigs and finely chop them. Juice the lemon. Mash the 8 tablespoons of butter in a medium bowl. Add the lemon juice, chopped rosemary, and salt and pepper to taste and mix well. Remove the butter from the bowl and form it into a log. Cut the log into 4 equal parts, wrap in plastic, and freeze.

On a large sheet of parchment or foil, toss the pearl onions with the remaining rosemary sprigs, 3 tablespoons of butter, and a bit of salt and pepper. Move the onions to one side of the paper, fold the paper over the onions, and crimp the edges to seal. Place the package on a baking sheet and roast for 40 minutes. Remove the package and let it cool.

Carefully open the onion packet and pour the juices into a medium skillet. When cool enough to handle, peel the pearl onions and place them in a skillet.

Heat a large oiled grill pan over medium-high heat. Salt and pepper the chops. Sear them, in batches if necessary, for 3 minutes on each side. (Alternatively, you can use a large oven-proof skillet and cook the chops in batches, in 2 to 3 tablespoons butter.) Return all the chops to the pan. Transfer the pan to the oven and roast for 10 minutes for medium (pink).

Transfer the chops to a platter and let them rest for 5 minutes. Add the vinegar to the skillet with the pearl onions and cook over medium heat, stirring, for a few minutes, until heated through. Taste for seasoning.

Remove the butter from the freezer and unwrap.

Place a chop on each plate and place a pat of the rosemary butter on each chop. Spoon the onions alongside the chops, decorate the plates with rosemary sprigs, and serve.

VENISON STEW WITH GOAT CHEESE JOHNNYCAKES

8 to 10 servings

My first cooking job was at a small Relais & Châteaux one-star restaurant in the Vosges region of northeastern France. It was a very old-fashioned place. We had no pastry chefs, no line cooks, no fancy equipment. When a customer ordered trout, it was my job to run out back and fish a frisky, uncooperative trout out of an enclosed pool. The restaurant also boasted a small fenced-in forest with its own population of deer. No, I did not have to run them down and do what was necessary. But I did learn how to braise venison Alsatian-style.

Later, when I was at Domaine Chandon in Napa Valley, chef Philippe Jeanty was my cohort in crime. He was a marvelously instinctual cook who knew more at age twenty than most cooks twice his age. This venison stew recipe reflects lessons from both France and Philippe.

Farm-raised venison is available from good butchers (usually frozen, but still acceptable) and from Canadian and New Zealand suppliers. Stews of venison are very delicate and tasty. This one is flavored with pork bones, root vegetables, and garlic. It is topped with johnnycakes, griddle-fried goat cheese pancakes made with cornmeal. They are a little like a light cheese crepe.

Many people overcook their root vegetables when they make stews. Don't be one of them!

Note that for best results, you should make the stock the day before and chill it overnight.

Stock

- 4 garlic heads
- 2–3 pounds pork bones (or ask your butcher to save you the venison bones)
- 3 onions
- 6 carrots
- 2 tablespoons olive oil
- 1 bouquet garni (see page 5)
- Kosher salt and freshly ground black pepper

Stew

- 4 pounds boneless stewing venison (or boneless beef chuck or pork shoulder)
- Kosher salt and freshly ground black pepper
- 5 chile peppers, such as jalapeños or serranos
- 3 onions
- 2 garlic heads
- 4 large leeks
- 8 tablespoons (1 stick) unsalted butter

6 tablespoons olive oil

1 750-ml bottle Cabernet Sauvignon

2 tablespoons chopped fresh rosemary

2 tablespoons fresh thyme leaves

3 large carrots

10 new potatoes or other small potatoes (about the size of golf balls)

8 turnips

6 parsnips

1 1-pound celery root

¼ pound thick-cut bacon

Johnnycakes

2 tablespoons unsalted butter, plus more for cooking

4 large eggs

1 cup milk, or more as needed

¾ cup all-purpose flour

¾ cup cornmeal, preferably Arrowhead

½ pound soft fresh goat cheese

Kosher salt and freshly ground black pepper

Garnish

3 shallots

Chopped fresh flat-leaf parsley

MAKE THE STOCK

Heat the oven to 400 degrees.

Halve the garlic heads horizontally and peel them. Put the bones, with the whole onions, carrots, and garlic, in a heavy roasting pan and drizzle with the olive oil. Roast, turning once or twice, until the bones are well browned, 20 to 30 minutes.

Transfer the bones and vegetables to a large pot. Skim off any accumulated fat from the roasting pan and place it over medium-high heat. Deglaze the pan with 4 cups water, stirring to scrape up the browned bits. Pour the liquid into the pot and add 4 quarts water. Bring to a boil, then turn the heat down until the stock just simmers. Add the bouquet garni and simmer for 3 hours, adding more water if necessary. Remove from the heat and let the stock cool.

Strain the stock into a bowl, cover, and refrigerate until chilled, or, preferably, overnight.

Scrape off any congealed fat from the stock. Pour into a saucepan and simmer to reduce to 2 quarts. Season with salt and pepper and set aside.

MAKE THE STEW

Cut the meat into 2-inch cubes and salt and pepper them. Don't remove any fat—you will need it in the cooking. Set aside.

Roast the chiles over medium-high heat on the stovetop or under a hot broiler, turning occasionally, until blackened and blistered all over. Place the chiles in a bowl, cover with plastic, and let them steam for 15 minutes.

Meanwhile, quarter the onions. Separate the garlic cloves and peel them. Trim the leeks, wash well, and slice them. Set aside.

Peel the chiles with your fingers (do not rinse) and stem and seed them. Thinly slice them.

Place a large enameled cast-iron casserole or Dutch oven over medium-high heat and add

3 tablespoons of the butter and 2 tablespoons of the olive oil. Brown the meat, in batches, on all sides; pour off the butter when it turns dark and add 3 more tablespoons of the butter and the remaining 4 tablespoons olive oil as needed. As it is browned, transfer the meat to a bowl with a slotted spoon.

Clean out the pot, add the remaining 2 tablespoons butter, and melt over medium heat. Add the onions and cook until soft, about 10 minutes. Add the garlic, chiles, and leeks and cook slowly, stirring occasionally, until the garlic is golden brown.

Discard as much fat as you can and return the meat to the pot. Pour in the Cabernet and stock, add the herbs, and bring the stew to a simmer. Cover and simmer gently over low heat for 4 hours, stirring occasionally, or until the meat is very tender.

MEANWHILE, MAKE THE BATTER FOR THE JOHNNYCAKES

Melt the 2 tablespoons butter in a small saucepan. Break the eggs into a large bowl and beat in the butter and milk. Whisk in the flour and cornmeal. Crumble the goat cheese and add to the batter. Let the batter sit, covered and refrigerated, for at least 1 hour. (The batter can be made up to 8 hours ahead.)

MEANWHILE, FINISH THE STEW

Peel the carrots and cut each one into 6 pieces. Peel the potatoes, turnips, parsnips, and celery root and cut into bite-sized pieces; as they're cut, place these vegetables in a bowl of cold water. Mince the shallots for the garnish and set aside.

Cut the bacon into 1-x-½-inch lardons. Fry in a large skillet until golden brown and crispy, about 8 minutes. Drain on paper towels.

When the meat is tender, bring a large saucepan of water to a boil. Reduce to a simmer, drain the vegetables, and add them to the simmering water; simmer until they're just tender, 6 minutes. Drain.

Add the vegetables and bacon to the stew. Taste carefully for seasoning. Keep warm over very low heat.

MAKE THE JOHNNYCAKES

Whisk the batter well, adding a few more tablespoons of milk if it seems too thick, and season with salt and pepper. Melt about 1 tablespoon butter on a griddle or in a large heavy skillet over medium heat. Add a ¼-cup measure of batter for each pancake and cook several at a time, turning once, until golden brown on both sides. Transfer to a plate and cover to keep warm while you cook the rest of the johnnycakes, adding about 1 tablespoon more butter to the skillet for each batch.

To serve, spoon the stew into bowls, sprinkle some parsley leaves over, and drape a johnnycake on top of each serving. Garnish with the shallots.

GRILLED RABBIT WITH ROASTED TOMATO SALSA

4 servings

For many years, recipes for rabbit languished in old cookbooks. Now we are rediscovering this meat: rabbit is versatile, flavorful, and satisfying. This is a true summer evening dish. The three parts of the recipe are done ahead of time, including the grilling of the rabbit. (The rabbit needs to marinate for at least 12 hours before grilling, so plan accordingly.)

The tomato salsa works well in many different guises. You can serve it with grilled chicken or even as a topping for grilled toasts. Serve the rabbit with buttered fettuccine.

14 shallots	8 large ripe plum tomatoes or drained canned plum tomatoes, preferably San Marzano
1 garlic head	
2 cups rosé wine	
1¼ cups olive oil	Kosher salt and freshly ground black pepper
8 fresh rosemary sprigs	
1 rabbit (3–4 pounds), cut into 8 serving pieces	2 tablespoons unsalted butter

Thinly slice 4 of the shallots. Separate the garlic head into cloves. Smash and peel half the cloves; reserve the rest. Combine 1 cup of the wine, the sliced shallots, smashed garlic, ¼ cup of the olive oil, and 4 rosemary sprigs in a large bowl. Place the rabbit pieces in the bowl, turning to coat. Cover with plastic and marinate in the refrigerator for at least 12 hours, or up to 2 days, turning several times.

Heat the oven to 500 degrees.

Cut the tomatoes in half. Sprinkle them with salt and pepper and place them cut side up in a roasting pan. Peel the remaining garlic cloves and 10 shallots. Scatter the whole garlic cloves and shallots over the tomatoes. Remove the leaves from the remaining 4 sprigs of rosemary, mince them, and sprinkle over the tomatoes. Finish by drizzling ½ cup of the olive oil over the tomatoes.

Place the pan in the hot oven and roast for 10 minutes. The tomatoes should begin to blister and then turn dark golden brown—watch carefully so they don't burn. Remove them from the oven, transfer to a bowl, and crush them roughly with a wooden spoon. Set aside.

Prepare a medium fire in a grill.

Remove the rabbit pieces from the marinade, reserving the marinade and the garlic and shallots for the sauce; discard the rosemary. Rub the rabbit with ¼ cup of the olive oil and season with salt and pepper. Grill over medium heat—rabbit has little fat and can dry out easily—until pink, 15 to 20 minutes; the meat should have reached an internal temperature of 150 degrees. Transfer to a platter and cover loosely to keep warm.

Meanwhile, heat the remaining ¼ cup olive oil in a medium skillet over medium-high heat. Add the garlic and shallots from the marinade and sauté until they're browned. Pour in the reserved marinade and the remaining 1 cup wine, bring to a boil, and boil for 10 minutes.

Strain the wine mixture into a clean saucepan. Boil to reduce to about 1 cup, then whisk in the butter, 1 tablespoon at a time.

Spoon the wine sauce over the rabbit and serve garnished with the tomato salsa.

FISH

TO GET THE FRESHEST POSSIBLE SPECIMENS, YOU NEED TO BE BOLD.

When I was six or seven years old, my family and I vacationed near the Carson Pass in the Sierra Nevadas. We went trout fishing for hours at a beautiful high Sierra lake. I was the lone victor, catching a huge trout on my trusty drop line. My maternal grandfather liked to take us fishing at the Tomales Bay pier, in a picturesque fishing village in Sonoma County. We fished for perch, rockfish, and caught an occasional crab, all for the sheer fun of pulling squiggling little fish out of the water.

Later, during my college days, we took camping excursions in the Grand Canyon of the Tuolumne in Yosemite Park. There I first caught some of the legendary golden trout. We cooked those beauties on an open fire.

Despite all my experiences as a fisherman, though, in my early years of cooking, I often found it difficult to select good fish and then choose an appropriate recipe. It would be wonderful to have an extraordinary fishmonger on the corner, but that's out of the question for most of us, unless we're lucky enough to live in a coastal village. Most supermarkets don't carry "fresh" fish, even if they guarantee it. In other countries, especially Portugal, Spain, France, and Italy, when the fishmonger has run out of fish, he's done for the day. But we insist on being able to buy fish seven days a week at any hour.

To get the freshest possible specimens, I learned, you need to be bold. Ask questions: Which fish arrived today? Which fish is line-caught? Which fish are wild? It may take a bit of persistence to get the best, but don't let the market tell you you can't examine your purchase before you pay for it.

All that said, here's what to look for: Whole fish should have clear, brilliant eyes. The skin should be pristine and glistening (this also applies to skin-on fillets). The gills should be ruby red, not covered with a gooey slime. The fish should feel firm to the touch—not rock hard—but it should offer some resistance. Although some fish, like bluefish, cod, and mackerel, are inherently soft, they still should push back a bit when pressed. Most important, the fish should smell sweet and briny, without a hint of ammonia or brackish water.

Compare different fish. If your heart was set on tuna but the wild salmon came in that day, there's no contest.

When cooking fish fillets, I tend to use two methods that achieve the same tender, moist, and perfectly cooked fish. For grilling, I recommend medium-high heat. Grill watchfully to achieve a golden brown crust. Cook until the fish is 80 percent cooked, then remove the fish to a plate and cover with a lid or an inverted plate. The fish will be perfectly cooked in exactly 10 minutes. You may ask, "What the hell is 80 percent cooked?" The answer is "rare," not raw. When you stop the grilling, the fish continues to cook. As the fish cools, the "carryover" heat penetrates the cooler interior, and after 10 minutes, you are left with a perfectly cooked fish. But you want to serve fish piping hot, so, after the 10 minutes are up, reheat the fish (save the juices on the plate) on the grill, covered, for 5 minutes. The fish will be cooked through, not rare, but *à point:* gloriously moist and succulent. For sautéing or roasting, the cooking method changes, but everything else is the same.

FISH

THE WAY TO COOK SALMON

You can cook any member of the salmon family in the same way. Here are some rules to go by.

TO SAUTÉ FILLETS: You don't want a hot pan. The oils in salmon flesh are delicate, and they turn nasty if the fish is cooked to a crisp. Cook fillets gently, in a mixture of butter and olive oil. If you want to bring in a bit more crispness, you can dredge the fillets in a mixture of fine cornmeal, flour, and sea salt. If the skin has been left on the fish, cook the skin side first, placing a weight, such as a small heavy skillet, on the fish to keep the skin flat so that it crisps evenly. Cooked in slightly sizzling butter-oil over medium heat, fillets will take about 3 minutes per side.

TO ROAST FILLETS: Slather the fillets with a flavored butter or olive oil, place in a roasting pan on some julienned or diced cooked vegetables or diced ripe tomatoes, and roast at 350 degrees for 8 minutes per inch of thickness.

TO ROAST A WHOLE 2- TO 3-POUND SALMON: Coating the fish in a salt–egg white crust ensures a particularly moist fish. The crust is easy: combine 4 cups kosher salt with 6 large egg whites and pack the mixture around the whole cleaned fish. Make a bed of about one third of the mixture in a large baking pan, set the fish on it, and put the rest of the salt around it, covering it completely. The fish will take exactly 5 minutes per pound at 400 degrees, plus 15 minutes to rest. Lightly tap the salt crust with a spoon to crack it, then lift the pieces off the fish.

TO COOK SALMON BY SMOKING: Make sure your kitchen is well ventilated. Marinate a whole fish or large fillet in a mixture of ¾ cup soy sauce, ½ cup sake, the juice of 2 limes, and 2 tablespoons grated peeled fresh ginger for 2 hours. Line a wok or heavy pan with a lid with heavy-duty aluminum foil. Put 1 cup raw rice, ½ cup packed brown sugar, ½ cup granulated sugar, and a cinnamon stick or 2 star anise in the wok. Cover the mixture with a sheet of foil pierced with holes and lay the salmon on a wire rack inside the wok. Cover the wok tightly and cover the lid with foil. Place over medium heat. The smoke will start almost immediately, and the fish will be perfectly smoked in no more than 20 minutes. Fantastic!

SALMON WITH ROASTED GARLIC CREAM

8 servings

One great side effect of having survived training with a French chef is the vocabulary of sauces one acquires. The mother of all sauces is the classic *sauce vin blanc,* white wine sauce. It's based on a broth made from fish bones and white wine with a few aromatic herbs, onions, mushrooms, and black pepper. The broth is cooked briefly, then strained, reduced to a glaze, enriched with cream, and then "mounted" with a little butter.

I was instructed in the intricacies of this sauce by the eminent master M. Fernand Chambrette, who had been a saucier at the famous Prunier fish restaurant in Paris and later had his own Michelin two-star restaurant.

I've augmented my sauce with roasted garlic, which provides unctuousness, making it possible to use half the cream that classic versions do.

Sauce

- 1 **large garlic head**
- 4 **tablespoons (½ stick) unsalted butter**
-    **Kosher salt and freshly ground**
        black pepper
- 1 **white onion**
- 1 **pound fish bones from nonoily**
        whitefish
- 4 **fresh parsley sprigs**
- 2 **bay leaves**
- 2 **cups dry white wine**
- ½ **cup heavy cream**

Salmon and vegetables

- ½ **pound green beans**
- 2 **medium turnips**
- 1 **bunch radishes**
- 1 **head radicchio**
- 1 **medium red bell pepper**
- 3 **tablespoons unsalted butter**
- 8 **6-ounce salmon fillets, preferably wild**
        Kosher salt and freshly ground
        black pepper
- ⅔ **cup peas**
- 2 **tablespoons olive oil**

MAKE THE SAUCE
Heat the oven to 350 degrees.

Pull the loose papery skin off the garlic, cut off the top of the garlic head, and place it on a sheet of foil. Dot the garlic with 2 tablespoons of the butter, sprinkle with salt and pepper, and wrap tightly in the foil. Place in a small baking dish and bake for 45 minutes, or until soft.

Meanwhile, thinly slice the onion. Rinse the fish bones thoroughly in cold water. Cut or chop into smaller pieces.

Place the onion in a large saucepan, add the remaining 2 tablespoons butter, and cook over low heat, stirring occasionally, for 5 minutes, or until the onion is softened. Add the bones, parsley, and bay leaves and cook, stirring, for

5 minutes. Pour in the wine, add 1 teaspoon black pepper, and bring to a simmer. Skim off the foam, reduce the heat, and simmer very gently for 25 minutes.

Strain the stock into another large saucepan. Bring to a boil and reduce the stock to about ½ cup liquid. Let cool.

When the garlic is soft, let cool slightly (leave the oven on), then remove it from the foil, cut it horizontally in half, and squeeze out the soft flesh; discard the skin.

Add the squeezed garlic to the reduced fish stock, then stir in the cream. Remove from the heat. (The sauce can be made 1 to 2 days in advance, covered, and refrigerated.)

MAKE THE SALMON AND VEGETABLES

Top and tail the beans. Peel the turnips and slice into quarters. Trim the radishes and halve them if they are large. Cut the radicchio into fine julienne. Stem and seed the pepper and cut it into ¼-inch-wide strips.

Bring two large saucepans of salted water to a boil.

Melt the butter in a small saucepan. Sprinkle the salmon with salt and pepper. Brush a rimmed baking sheet with some of the melted butter. Rub the fish with the remaining butter and place it on the baking sheet. Bake for 10 minutes.

Meanwhile, cook the beans, turnips, and radishes in one saucepan of boiling water for 5 to 7 minutes, until crisp-tender. Cook the pepper strips and peas in the other pan of boiling water for about 3 minutes, or until the pepper strips are crisp-tender. Drain the vegetables, place in a large skillet, and set aside.

When the salmon is done (springy to the touch), place it on a large ovenproof platter. Set aside in a warm spot. (Leave the oven on.)

Rewarm the sauce over low heat. Meanwhile, place the skillet with the vegetables over medium heat and add the olive oil. Add the radicchio, season with salt and pepper to taste, and heat through, tossing occasionally.

Surround the salmon with the vegetables and pour the sauce over the top of the salmon. Heat in the oven for 2 minutes. Serve at once.

SAUTÉED MONKFISH WITH SPAGHETTI SQUASH

4 servings

Monkfish is sometimes called the poor man's lobster, due to its meaty texture and flavor that is reminiscent of shellfish. In fact, shellfish is a large part of a monkfish's diet. With its huge head, this is a grotesquely ugly fish, but the skinned fillets are quite beautiful. Since it loses its firmness quickly, monkfish needs to be extremely fresh. Only 30 percent of the whole fish is edible—its tail—but it's usually relatively inexpensive.

Spaghetti squash is a wonder: the cooked squash shreds into spaghetti-like strands, which you can toss with plenty of butter to create a nest for the monkfish.

1 pound monkfish fillets, 1 inch thick
Kosher salt and freshly ground
   black pepper
Olive oil
1 medium spaghetti squash
   (about 2 pounds)

6 tablespoons (¾ stick) unsalted butter
2 lemons
½ cup fish broth or dry white wine
8 fresh sage leaves

Heat the oven to 400 degrees.

Cut away any membranes from the monkfish, rinse, and pat dry. Slice the monkfish into 8 equal pieces. Flatten each one slightly with the side of a large knife, and salt and pepper them. Brush a plate with olive oil. Place the fish on the plate, turning to coat lightly, cover, and refrigerate.

Cut the squash lengthwise in half and remove the strings and seeds. Dot the halves with 2 tablespoons of the butter and salt and pepper to taste. Place on a baking sheet and roast the squash for 20 to 30 minutes, or until tender. Use the tines of a large fork to flick out the tangled strands from the squash.

Heat the broiler. Zest 1 lemon and juice them both.

Melt the remaining 4 tablespoons butter in a large skillet over medium-high heat, then cook until it turns a hazelnut color. Add the fish, in batches if necessary, and cook for 2 minutes on each side, or until just cooked through. Remove the fish and place on a baking sheet.

Add the broth or wine to the hot skillet, bring to a boil, and reduce by half. Lower the heat to medium and add the squash, lemon zest and juice, and sage leaves and cook, stirring occasionally, for 5 minutes. Taste for seasoning, and form 2 nests of squash on each of four plates.

Meanwhile, reheat the monkfish under the broiler for 1 minute, or until hot. Place on the squash nests and serve immediately.

TUNA STEAKS WITH GINGER–BLACK PEPPER SAUCE

4 servings

Tuna is the steak of the fish family. It's plentiful in all our ocean waters and fished all around our shoreline. The late summer produces the bulk of the year's catch, but the availability of the Southern Hemisphere's catch makes it possible to serve fresh tuna year-round.

When you cook large pieces of tuna, either on a grill or in a skillet, use a large wide spatula, because once cooked, the fish tends to flake a bit. For this recipe, I use 2-inch-thick tuna steaks; you may need to call the fish market ahead to order this cut.

Marinating the tuna for just half an hour will transform the flavors tremendously.

2 limes
3 tablespoons toasted sesame oil
3 tablespoons rice wine vinegar
1 tablespoon soy sauce
2 tablespoons grated peeled
    fresh ginger
¼ cup coriander seeds
4 6-ounce tuna steaks, 2 inches thick

8 fresh cilantro sprigs
2 red bell peppers
2 poblano chiles
4 tablespoons (½ stick) cold
    unsalted butter
2 tablespoons lightly cracked
    black peppercorns
2 tablespoons olive oil

Juice the limes. Combine half the lime juice, the sesame oil, vinegar, soy sauce, 1 tablespoon of the ginger, and the coriander seeds in a small bowl and whisk together until well blended.

Place the tuna steaks in a baking dish large enough to hold them in a single layer. Add the marinade and 4 of the cilantro sprigs, turning to coat the tuna. Let the tuna marinate at room temperature for 30 minutes.

Core and stem the peppers and chiles and cut them into 1-x-2-inch triangles. Set aside.

Melt 2 tablespoons of the butter in a small saucepan over medium heat. Add the peppercorns and cook for 2 to 3 minutes, until fragrant.

Lift the tuna from the marinade and set aside on a plate. Strain the marinade and add it to the peppercorn saucepan. Add the remaining lime juice and cook until the liquid is slightly reduced. Turn off the heat and cover to keep warm.

Heat the olive oil in a large heavy skillet over medium heat. Add the peppers and chiles and sauté just until tender, 7 to 8 minutes. Remove from the pan with a slotted spoon and set aside on a plate, covered to keep warm.

Add the tuna to the pan and cook, turning once, until medium-rare, 2 to 3 minutes per side.

Meanwhile, reheat the sauce just to a simmer. Off the heat, whisk in the remaining 2 tablespoons cold butter, 1 tablespoon at a time. Add the remaining tablespoon of ginger and cover to keep warm.

Arrange the sautéed peppers and chiles and the tuna on serving plates and top with the ginger–black pepper sauce. Garnish with the remaining cilantro sprigs, and serve.

TUNA WITH PEANUT-CHILE SAUCE

4 servings

You can cook big pieces, or "loins," of tuna almost like a filet of beef. Let the fish come to room temperature before cooking, and let the tuna rest after cooking just as you would any roast. This helps to resettle the juices inside. The peanut sauce for this dish has a wonderfully silky, dense texture, lightened with a little lime and butter and given a jolt by roasted jalapeño chile.

You will probably have to order the tuna "roast" in advance.

24 ounces tuna, cut from the loin (about 15 inches long)	2 limes
⅓ cup plus ¼ cup olive oil, plus more for rubbing the tuna	1 garlic clove
Kosher salt and freshly ground black pepper	4 tablespoons (½ stick) unsalted butter, at room temperature
1 jalapeño chile	½ cup chopped fresh cilantro, plus small sprigs for garnish
1 cup raw peanuts (available at health food stores)	4 plum tomatoes
1 red bell pepper	2 tablespoons sherry vinegar
	6 small zucchini (4–6 inches long)

Rub the tuna with a little olive oil and sprinkle with salt and pepper. Set aside on a plate.

Heat the oven to 400 degrees.

Roast the jalapeño over medium-high heat on the stovetop or under a hot broiler, turning occasionally, until blackened and blistered all over. Place the jalapeño in a bowl, cover with plastic, and let steam for 15 minutes.

Meanwhile, toss the peanuts on a baking sheet with a little olive oil and a sprinkle of water. Roast in the oven, stirring occasionally, for 8 minutes, or until golden brown. Drain the peanuts on paper towels. Increase the oven temperature to 425 degrees.

Peel the jalapeño with your fingers (do not rinse), stem, seed, and cut into strips. Stem and seed the bell pepper and cut it into tiny dice. Juice the limes.

With a mortar and pestle or a food processor, mash ¾ cup of the peanuts with the jalapeño and the garlic clove, then dribble in 2 tablespoons of the olive oil, mashing it into the peanuts. Cut the butter into chunks and blend it thoroughly into the peanut mixture, using the lime juice to facilitate matters. Stir in the chopped cilantro and diced red pepper, and season with salt and with pepper if necessary. Transfer to a bowl.

Dice the tomatoes. Whisk the vinegar with salt and pepper to taste in a medium bowl. Whisk in the ⅓ cup olive oil. Stir in the tomatoes. Set aside.

Slice the zucchini lengthwise into strips. Heat the remaining 2 tablespoons olive oil in a large skillet. Add the zucchini, season lightly with salt and pepper, and sauté until just tender. Keep warm.

Meanwhile, place the tuna on a baking sheet and roast for 4 minutes on each side, about 12 minutes total. The outside of the tuna will be cooked, but the center will be very rare. Remove the tuna to a platter and let rest for 5 minutes.

Slice the tuna into 4 equal pieces. Place a mound of sautéed zucchini on each plate. Sprinkle with the tomato vinaigrette, then the remaining peanuts. Place the slices of tuna against the zucchini, then top each piece of tuna with some peanut sauce. Garnish with cilantro sprigs and serve.

GRAND RED SNAPPER STEW

4 to 6 servings

Some of the most sensuous fish stews in the world are found on the Riviera, rivaled only by the fantastic stews of Spain, especially Catalonia, and those of Provence. This dish is inspired by those recipes. It's made with red snapper, which is widely fished in our waters. You could substitute halibut, cod, grouper, or monkfish.

Stew

4   fennel bulbs with fronds
2   large red onions
4   garlic cloves
1   celery stalk
1   large carrot
1   large leek
¼   cup plus 1 tablespoon olive oil
¼   cup fresh flat-leaf parsley leaves
2   cups dry white wine
2   bay leaves
1   teaspoon saffron threads, plus
      about ¼ teaspoon for garnish

Kosher salt and freshly ground
      black pepper
2   pounds red snapper fillets
4   tablespoons (½ stick) unsalted butter
2   medium ripe tomatoes

Garlic toasts

4–6   ½-inch-thick slices baguette
        or sourdough bread
½   garlic clove
      Olive oil, for brushing

MAKE THE STEW

Trim the fennel, reserving a few feathery fennel fronds for garnishing. Halve the fennel bulbs and thinly slice crosswise. Cut the onions lengthwise into thin strips. Thinly slice the garlic. Slice the celery stalk into 1-inch pieces. Peel the carrot and cut into ¼-inch-thick coins. Trim the leek, wash well, and slice.

Heat ¼ cup of the olive oil in a large enameled cast-iron casserole or Dutch oven over medium heat. Add the fennel, onions, garlic, celery, carrot, and leek and sauté for 10 to 15 minutes, stirring often. Stir in the parsley, then pour in

the wine and 2 cups cold water, add the bay leaves and saffron, and bring to a simmer. Reduce the heat to low and simmer for 45 minutes. Turn off the heat and discard the bay leaves.

MEANWHILE, MAKE THE GARLIC TOASTS

Heat the oven to 350 degrees.

Place the bread on a baking sheet and lightly toast in the oven for about 5 minutes, or until golden. Rub each piece with the garlic half and brush with oil.

FINISH THE STEW

Salt and pepper the red snapper and cut into bite-sized pieces. Melt the butter in a large skillet over medium-high heat. Add the snapper to the skillet, skin side down, and cook the pieces for 1 minute. Add the snapper to the stew. Bring the stew to a simmer.

Slice the tomatoes into ⅛-inch-thick rounds and divide them among four to six bowls. Place 1 of the garlic toasts in each of the bowls and sprinkle with the remaining tablespoon of olive oil. Ladle the stew into the bowls and garnish with the reserved fennel fronds and saffron.

CURRIED CATFISH WITH APPLE-CORN FRITTERS

6 servings

Farm-raised catfish is readily available, and it's tender, flaky, and moist. Some find the flavor a bit earthy, but I think that's a positive attribute.

This recipe calls for the fish to be fried in a curry-cornmeal mixture. This is a wonderful way to add a subtle Indian spiciness to the fish without masking its intrinsic flavor. The spice mixture works well with other fish, and equally well with chicken.

The tart apple and corn fritters are a cinch. The fritters are good on their own, with nothing but a dollop of sour cream. A simple pan sauce made with a little white wine, a combination of citrus juices, and butter brings everything together.

1 lemon	¼ cup plus 2 tablespoons all-purpose flour
1 lime	2 bunches watercress
4 crisp, tart apples (Pippins, Gravensteins, or Granny Smiths)	About 4 cups corn oil or peanut oil, for deep-frying
1 orange	½ cup dry white wine
2 ears corn	6 6-ounce skinless catfish fillets
About 12 tablespoons (1½ sticks) unsalted butter	1 cup milk
Kosher salt and freshly ground black pepper	1 cup cornmeal
3 large eggs	¼ cup curry powder
¼ bottle (6 tablespoons) Anchor Steam beer or other good lager	3 tablespoons minced fresh chives, for garnish (optional)

Halve the lemon and lime. Peel and core the apples. Cut them into ¼-inch cubes and place in a bowl. Squeeze a little lemon and lime juice over the pieces and toss well.

Juice the lemon, lime, and orange and combine the juices in a small bowl. Set aside.

Husk the corn and cut the kernels from the cobs. Melt 2 tablespoons of the butter in a medium skillet and sauté the corn just until tender, adding a little salt and pepper. Let the corn cool.

Separate the eggs, putting the yolks in one medium bowl and the whites in another medium bowl. Add the beer to the yolks and whisk in the ¼ cup flour until well combined. Add the corn and apples and fold everything together carefully. Set aside.

Trim the watercress, rinse, and dry. Cover and refrigerate.

Heat the oven to 250 degrees.

Heat the oil in a large deep pot over medium-high heat to 325 degrees. Meanwhile, beat the egg whites until they form soft peaks. Stir a little of the egg whites into the batter, then fold in the rest of the whites. Season with salt and pepper. Add 2 or 3 tablespoons of the batter to the hot oil for each fritter and cook until golden brown on the first side, about 2 minutes. Turn and cook about a minute more, until golden brown. Remove with a slotted spoon and drain on paper towels, then place on a baking sheet and keep the cooked fritters warm in the oven. Continue until all are cooked.

Combine the wine and the reserved citrus juices in a saucepan and boil to reduce the mixture to ½ cup. Turn off the heat.

Place a large cast-iron skillet over medium heat. While the skillet heats, season the catfish with salt and pepper. Pour the milk into a shallow bowl. Mix the cornmeal, curry, and the remaining 2 tablespoons flour in another shallow bowl. Season with salt and pepper. Dip the catfish in the milk, then dredge each fillet in the cornmeal-curry mixture and set on a plate.

Add 2 tablespoons of the butter to the hot skillet. When the butter is golden brown and foamy, add 2 or 3 of the catfish fillets and fry until crispy and browned, about 2 minutes per side, adjusting the heat as necessary. Drain briefly on paper towels, then transfer to a platter and keep warm. Wipe out the remnants of cornmeal and burned fat in the pan and cook the remaining fillets, using the butter as needed for the pan.

Reheat the citrus juice mixture and gradually whisk in the remaining 4 tablespoons butter. Add salt and pepper as needed.

Arrange a bed of watercress on each of six serving plates. Place the catfish fillets on the watercress and spoon the sauce over the catfish. Surround with the fritters, scattering with the minced chives, if using, and serve right away.

GRILLED SWORDFISH WITH BLOOD ORANGE SAUCE

4 servings

The meaty quality of swordfish needs a strong accompaniment. Blood oranges are more deeply flavored than regular oranges, rich, and not cloyingly sweet. The season for blood oranges is the late winter months, so that's when this recipe should be pulled out. You can substitute halibut, marlin, or shark for the swordfish, and regular oranges for the blood oranges.

6 blood oranges	½ cup chopped fresh cilantro
1 Anaheim or poblano chile	4 8-ounce swordfish steaks,
1 small jicama	about 1 inch thick
1 small red onion	6 tablespoons (¾ stick) cold
3 tablespoons olive oil, plus more	unsalted butter
for rubbing the swordfish	
Kosher salt and freshly ground	
black pepper	

Zest 1 of the oranges using a zester or vegetable peeler. Juice the orange and place the juice in a medium bowl. If you used a peeler, cut the zest into very thin strips. Set aside.

Slice the tops and bottoms off the remaining 5 oranges, exposing the fruit. Stand each orange on a cutting board and, using a sharp paring knife, following the contours of the fruit, slice off the peel in strips from top to bottom, making sure to remove the bitter white pith. To remove the sections, hold each orange in the palm of your hand and, working over the bowl of orange juice, gently slice along each membrane to release the whole segments. Put the orange sections in another bowl. Cover and refrigerate.

Prepare a medium-hot fire in a grill.

Roast the chile over medium-high heat on the stovetop or under a hot broiler, turning occasionally, until blackened and blistered all over. Place the chile in a bowl, cover with plastic wrap, and let steam for 15 minutes.

Meanwhile, peel the jicama and cut it into ½-inch dice. Slice the onion lengthwise into thin strips.

Peel the chile pepper with your fingers (do not rinse); stem, seed, and dice it.

Combine half the orange juice and the olive oil in a small bowl. Stir in the chile, jicama, and onion. Season with salt and pepper to taste.

Add half the orange sections to the bowl with the jicama mixture and toss. Mix in half the cilantro. Divide the salad among four plates.

Rub the swordfish steaks with olive oil, then salt and pepper them to taste. Grill the swordfish steaks, turning once, until they're just cooked through, about 4 minutes per side.

Meanwhile, combine the rest of the orange juice with the orange zest and the remaining cilantro in a medium saucepan and bring to a simmer. Whisk in the butter 1 tablespoon at a time. Add the remaining orange sections and taste, adding salt and pepper if necessary.

Place the swordfish steaks on the salad and drizzle with the orange sauce. Serve at once.

SARDINES WITH GREEN SALSA

4 first-course servings or 2 main-course servings

The lowly sardine is inexpensive, yet tastes like a true luxury food. In Spain, Portugal, and France, it's regarded as a delicacy. The fish need to be impeccably fresh. These can be panfried or grilled, but gently and quickly.

Salsa

3	anchovy fillets
2	garlic cloves
1	cup loosely packed fresh basil leaves
1	cup loosely packed fresh flat-leaf parsley leaves
¼	teaspoon red pepper flakes
1	cup olive oil
	Kosher salt and freshly ground black pepper

Sardines

1–2	lemons
1	lime
16	extremely fresh whole sardines (about 6 ounces each)
	Olive oil, for rubbing the sardines
	Kosher salt and cracked black peppercorns
16	small fresh rosemary sprigs
	Olive oil, if panfrying the sardines

MAKE THE SALSA

With a mortar and pestle or a blender, puree the anchovies, garlic, herbs, and pepper flakes. Slowly drizzle in the olive oil, blending well. Season to taste with salt, if necessary, and pepper.

Using a vegetable peeler or a paring knife, remove 16 thin strips of zest from the lemon(s); set aside. Halve the lime and 1 lemon; set aside.

Grasp the gills of each sardine below the head and pull them out. If the innards don't come away with the gills, slide your index finger into the cavity and pull them out. Rinse the sardines well under cold water, rubbing off the scales, then wipe dry with paper towels. Rub with a little olive oil and salt and a little cracked pepper. Put a sprig of rosemary and a slice of lemon zest into each sardine cavity. Keep cold.

If you are planning to grill the sardines, prepare a medium-hot fire.

TO GRILL THE SARDINES

If you have a grill basket, place the sardines in the basket. Grill them, turning once, for 1 to 2 minutes on each side, or until just cooked through.

TO PANFRY THE SARDINES

Heat ½ inch olive oil in a large skillet over medium-high heat. Fry the sardines in batches, turning once, for 1 to 2 minutes per side, or until just cooked through. Transfer to a platter.

Divide the fish among serving plates. Drizzle with the salsa, squeeze a little lemon and lime juice over the sardines, and serve.

SPICY SWORDFISH

4 servings

Pairing milder fish with chiles can overwhelm their delicate flavor, but large meaty fish such as rock cod, salmon, and swordfish benefit from the zesty heat. Controlling the heat is easier if you combine sweet bell peppers with hot chiles, as I do here in this complementary sauce.

1   jalapeño chile
1   red bell pepper
4   6-ounce swordfish steaks,
       about 1 inch thick
¼   cup olive oil, plus more for
       rubbing the swordfish
     Kosher salt and freshly ground
       black pepper

10 fresh basil leaves
1   tablespoon fresh marjoram, oregano,
       or flat-leaf parsley leaves
1   tablespoon minced fresh chives
2   teaspoons fresh thyme leaves
3   garlic cloves
¾   cup crème fraîche

Roast the jalapeño and bell pepper over medium-high heat on the stovetop or under a hot broiler, turning occasionally, until blackened and blistered all over. Place the chile and pepper in a bowl, cover with plastic, and let steam for 15 minutes.

Meanwhile, rub the swordfish steaks with a little olive oil, season with salt and pepper, and place on a plate. Chop the basil leaves.

Peel the jalapeño and bell pepper with your fingers (do not rinse) and stem them. Seed the bell pepper. Place the jalapeño, bell pepper, herbs, garlic, crème fraîche, and the ¼ cup olive oil in a blender and puree. Taste for seasoning, adding salt to taste and pepper if needed. Transfer to a small bowl.

Heat the broiler. Place the swordfish on the broiler pan and broil for 2 to 3 minutes per side, until just cooked through.

Transfer the swordfish to plates, drizzle with the sauce, and serve.

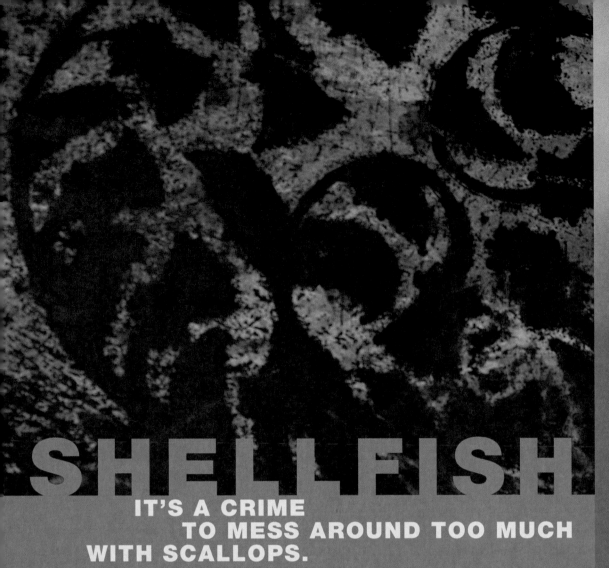

SHELLFISH

IT'S A CRIME TO MESS AROUND TOO MUCH WITH SCALLOPS.

I thought I knew my seafood. After all, I had worked in Hawaii and encountered giant wild blue shrimp from the island of Molokai. I had lived, studied, and worked in France, where I'd managed to consume quantities of sea urchins, oysters, baby shrimp, sea slugs, lobsters, huge crabs, and periwinkles. But at Michael's, the toniest place in Los Angeles, I was thrown for a loop when the first soft-shell crabs arrived from Maryland.

The wackiest of all the wacky crew in the kitchen was my sous-chef the inestimable Billy Flug, who hailed from Boston. Billy had a gift for cooking, notwithstanding his penchant for dressing in dubious chef's attire. Just the week before, I had found him in the kitchen clad in a makeshift toga (the largest tablecloth we owned), an apron, shoes, and nothing else. But that day, Billy calmly ducked out the side door, borrowed some extremely sharp scissors from the haberdasher next door, and quietly gave me a lesson in soft-shell crab butchery. I've been making up for lost time ever since, serving soft-shells in soups, sandwiches, and pasta and over spicy vegetables.

The shellfish preparations in this chapter will help to expand your crustacean vocabulary. These recipes are also good platforms from which to begin your own experimentation. The best advice I can give is to make sure your shellfish is of impeccable freshness and, in the case of lobsters and crabs, really kicking! Clean clams, mussels, oysters, and scallops

SHELLFISH

of all sand and particles. Save the shells from crabs or lobsters to make a seafood stock, which is great for spontaneous stews, soups, sauces, and pastas.

Obviously, living near a seashore gives you an advantage, but lately supermarkets everywhere have begun maintaining tanks for lobsters and crabs and are meeting the growing demand for shellfish and making a greater effort to carry a wider array.

SAUTÉED SHRIMP WITH LEEKS AND ROASTED PEANUTS

6 servings

This is one of those dishes I arrived at through sheer inspiration in the heat of the moment, at my restaurant Bud's in New York City. It's a triumphant combination of tropical and European flavors: shrimp, stir-fried with peanuts, soy, lime, and ginger, served on top of fried rice cakes and garnished with crispy deep-fried leeks.

1	medium onion
¼	cup olive oil, plus more for the baking sheet
¾	cup basmati rice
	Kosher salt and freshly ground black pepper
¼	pound leeks
2	pounds large shrimp (16–20 per pound) in the shell
1	cup dry white wine

2	serrano chiles
1	lime
½	lemon
	About 4 cups corn oil or peanut oil, for deep-frying
1	cup roasted unsalted peanuts
¼	cup julienned peeled fresh ginger
¼	cup soy sauce

Mince the onion. Heat 2 tablespoons of the olive oil in a medium skillet over medium-high heat. Add the onion and basmati rice, season with salt and pepper to taste, and cook, stirring, for 5 minutes, or until the onion is softened and the rice is slightly toasted. Add 1 cup water and bring to a boil. Lower the heat, cover, and cook for 30 minutes, or until the rice is tender.

Spread the rice out on an oiled baking sheet and allow to cool.

Wash and trim the leeks. Separate the green parts from the white. Julienne the green portions and slice the white portions into thin rounds.

Remove the shells from the shrimp and place the shells in a medium saucepan. Cover and refrigerate the shrimp. Add the leek whites, wine, and 1 cup water to the shrimp shells, bring to a simmer, and simmer for 30 minutes. Strain and reserve the stock.

Stem and mince the chiles. Juice the lime and the lemon half. Form the cooled rice into six flat 1-inch-thick cakes; set aside.

Heat the corn or peanut oil in a large deep pot to 350 degrees.

Deep-fry the julienned leek greens for 1 to 2 minutes, or until golden. Remove with a slotted

spoon, drain on paper towels, and salt lightly. Leave the oil on the heat.

Deep-fry the rice cakes in the oil, in batches if necessary, for 3 to 4 minutes per side, until golden brown. Remove with a slotted spoon and drain on paper towels; keep warm in the oven.

In a large heavy skillet, heat the remaining 2 tablespoons olive oil to almost smoking. Add the shrimp and cook, stirring, for 1 minute. Add the peanuts, ginger, and chiles and cook, stirring, for 1 minute. Add the shrimp stock, citrus juices, and soy sauce and simmer gently for 3 minutes, or just until the shrimp are firm. Taste for seasoning, adding salt and pepper if needed, and keep warm.

Arrange the rice cakes on a platter. Top with the shrimp, scatter the deep-fried leek greens over all, and serve.

SEA SCALLOPS ON SWEET ONIONS

4 servings

It's a crime to mess around too much with scallops. Searing them and arranging them on top of a tender bed of slow-cooked onions is all they require.

Start the meal with a simple soup or a light crisp appetizer. This dish is rich, so you don't want to serve anything too complex before it.

1 pound very fresh large sea scallops

1 cup dry white wine

2 pounds sweet onions, such as Vidalia

9 tablespoons (1 stick plus 1 tablespoon) unsalted butter

Kosher salt and freshly ground black pepper

2 tablespoons chopped fresh flat-leaf parsley

Remove the small tough muscle from the side of each scallop and reserve; cover and refrigerate the scallops. Put the scallop scraps in a small saucepan, add the wine, and bring to a simmer. Reduce the heat and simmer gently for 20 minutes. Strain the liquid into a small bowl.

Slice the onions lengthwise in half, then slice them crosswise as thin as possible. Melt 5 tablespoons of the butter in a large heavy saucepan over medium heat. Add the onions and a little salt and pepper and cook over very low heat, stirring often, for 40 minutes, or until the onions are creamy and luscious.

Add the reduced wine and continue to cook until the onions are almost melted but have not colored at all. Keep warm.

Pat the scallops dry and salt and pepper them. Melt 2 tablespoons of the butter in a large skillet over medium heat. Put half the scallops in the pan and cook, without disturbing them, for about 3 minutes, or until the scallop bottoms brown and release easily from the skillet. Turn with tongs and brown the other side. Transfer the scallops to a plate and cover loosely to keep warm. Melt the remaining 2 tablespoons butter and brown the remaining scallops. Transfer them to the plate with the other scallops.

Place the onions on a warm platter. Arrange the scallops on top of the onions, sprinkle with the parsley, and serve promptly.

SEA SCALLOP BROCHETTES WITH ALMOND-CHILE SAUCE

8 servings

Scallops and radishes are grilled on bamboo skewers and drizzled with a spicy almond-chile sauce. Skewering the scallops prevents them from dropping between the grill grates, and using two skewers for each brochette steadies them, holding them flat so they grill evenly.

Make sure your scallops smell sweetly of the sea. They should be firm and resilient.

2	pounds (24) sea scallops
¼	cup olive oil, plus more as needed
4	limes
12	medium radishes
2	large tomatoes
1	garlic clove
1½	cups raw whole almonds (available in health food stores)
1–2	jalapeño chiles
½	cup peanut oil
	Kosher salt and freshly ground black pepper
2	heads radicchio or Belgian endive (optional)
¾	cup loosely packed chopped fresh cilantro

Heat the oven to 375 degrees.

Meanwhile, soak sixteen 12-inch bamboo skewers in water for 30 minutes.

Pull off and discard the small tough muscle from the side of each scallop. Toss the scallops with a little olive oil, cover, and refrigerate.

Juice 2 of the limes. Cut the remaining 2 into wedges. Trim and halve the radishes. Finely chop the tomatoes. Mince the garlic. Set aside.

Spread the almonds on a baking sheet and roast in the oven for about 10 minutes, stirring occasionally, until golden. Remove and set aside to cool.

Roast the chiles over medium-high heat on the stovetop or under a hot broiler, turning occasionally, until blackened and blistered all over. Place them in a bowl, cover with plastic, and let them steam for 15 minutes.

Peel the chiles with your fingers (do not rinse), then stem and seed. Mince them.

MAKE THE ALMOND SAUCE
Combine the peanut oil, the ¼ cup olive oil, the garlic, and almonds in a food processor and pulse to a chunky puree. Add half the lime juice and the chile and puree until smooth. Taste and add more chile and/or lime juice if necessary,

tasting carefully as you go. Add half the toma-toes and process to a puree. Season with salt and pepper. Transfer to a bowl. If the sauce is too thick, stir in a little warm water to loosen it.

GRILL THE BROCHETTES
Prepare a medium-hot fire in a grill.

Prepare the brochettes, using two skewers side by side and ½ inch apart for each one. Thread a scallop onto the parallel skewers, then thread a radish half onto the skewers. Continue, alternating the scallops and radishes, using 3 scallops and 3 radish halves per skewer. Drizzle the scallops and radishes with olive oil and sprinkle with salt and pepper. Set aside on a platter.

If using the radicchio or endive, cut lengthwise in half. Poach in simmering water for 1 minute. Drain and refresh in a bowl of ice water, then drain again and pat dry. Coat with olive oil and season with salt and pepper.

In a small bowl, toss the remaining tomatoes with a little cilantro, olive oil, the remaining lime juice, and salt.

Grill the scallops, turning once, until they're nicely charred on both sides. Don't be timid—get the scallops nice and crispy. If using the radicchio or endive, grill at the same time, turning occasionally, until well browned.

Arrange the radicchio or endive, if using, on a large (clean) platter. Put the skewers on the platter and dribble the almond-chile sauce over the skewers. Scatter the tomatoes and the remaining cilantro over the platter, decorate with the lime wedges, and serve.

PISMO BEACH CLAM RAGOUT

2 to 4 servings

In days long gone by, Pismo Beach yielded vast quantities of clams that were large, sweet, and delicious. This is my ode to those bygone clams. Serve with toasted garlic bread.

2 pounds littleneck clams

4 ears corn

2 sweet onions, such as Vidalia

3 tablespoons unsalted butter

Kosher salt and freshly ground
   black pepper

1 cup Sauvignon Blanc or other
   dry white wine

Wash the clams thoroughly. Shuck the corn and cut the kernels off the cobs with a sharp knife. Thinly slice the onions crosswise into rings.

Melt the butter in a large deep skillet over high heat. Add the corn and onions, season with salt and pepper, and cook, stirring, for 3 minutes. Add the clams and wine, cover, and cook until the clams open wide, 8 to 10 minutes. Discard any clams that do not open. Serve hot.

WARM LOBSTER TACOS WITH GUACAMOLE

6 to 8 servings

Practically from the very first time I cooked New England lobsters, I began to imagine their meat tucked inside a soft corn tortilla, smothered with red or green salsa, topped with shredded lettuce, and served with guacamole on the side. When I finally put this little fantasy dish to the test, the results were even better than I had imagined. Lobster is so rich that it stands up well to the strong flavors of chiles and lime, or grilled onions, tomatillos, and the like.

2	1½-pound live lobsters	3	poblano chiles
1	medium onion	2	avocados
4	medium tomatoes	1	lime
2	shallots		Sea salt
3	jalapeño chiles	16	corn tortillas
20	fresh cilantro sprigs	2	tablespoons olive oil

Bring a large pot of salted water to a boil. Plunge the lobsters into the water, cover, and boil for 10 minutes (the lobsters will not be fully cooked). Remove the lobsters and let cool. Reserve 2 cups of the cooking water.

Remove all the meat from the lobsters, saving the shells. Slice the lobster meat, cover, and refrigerate. Chop or cut the shells into smaller pieces.

Chop the onion. Combine the onion, lobster shells, and the reserved lobster cooking liquid in a large saucepan and bring to a boil, then reduce the heat to low and simmer, covered, for 1 hour.

Strain the lobster broth, pour it into a clean saucepan, and boil to reduce it to ¼ cup. Remove from the heat.

Finely chop the tomatoes and place in a small bowl. Dice the shallots and toss them with the tomatoes. Mince 1 of the jalapeños and add to the tomatoes. Remove the leaves from 5 of the cilantro sprigs, chop them, and add to the tomato mixture, tossing well. Moisten the mixture with the reduced lobster broth.

Roast the poblano chiles and the remaining 2 jalapeños over medium-high heat on the stovetop or under a hot broiler, turning occasionally, until blackened and blistered all over. Place them in a bowl, cover with plastic, and let them steam for 15 minutes.

Meanwhile, heat the oven to 300 degrees.

Remove the leaves from the remaining cilantro sprigs and chop them. Peel and pit the avocados and scrape the flesh into a bowl. Cut the lime in half and squeeze the juice of one of the halves over the avocados. Mash the avocados, adding sea salt to taste. Add half of the cilantro. Taste the guacamole for seasoning, adding more salt and/or lime juice if necessary.

Peel the chiles with your fingers (do not rinse). Stem, seed, and cut into strips.

Wrap the tortillas in a damp kitchen towel and set on a plate, or wrap in aluminum foil, and heat in the oven for 10 minutes.

Heat the olive oil in a large skillet over medium heat. Add the lobster meat and chile strips. When the mixture is hot, begin to assemble the tacos. Spoon some guacamole across the center of a tortilla. Add some lobster meat, then some tomato salsa, and finally a sprinkling of the remaining chopped cilantro. Fold the tortilla loosely over the filling and place on a platter. Repeat until all the tacos are made. Serve at once.

BROILED LOBSTER WITH ZUCCHINI AND CHILE BUTTER

8 servings

Here's an uncomplicated way to cook lobster. The spicy butter is spectacular with the lobster meat.

1	jalapeño chile, preferably red	½	lemon
6	tablespoons (¾ stick) unsalted butter, at room temperature	4	1½-pound lobsters
1	fresh rosemary sprig	8–12	medium zucchini
	Kosher salt and freshly ground black pepper	¼	cup olive oil

Bring a large pot of salted water to a boil.

Meanwhile, stem, seed, and coarsely chop the chile. Puree the chile with the butter in a small food processor or a blender. Remove the rosemary leaves, finely chop, and add them to the chile butter. Season with salt and pepper and squeeze in a little lemon juice to taste.

To kill the lobsters, one at a time, drop each lobster into the boiling water, cover, and boil for 3 minutes. Remove and let cool.

Split the lobsters lengthwise in half. Crack their claws lightly with a meat mallet. Divide the butter into 8 portions and rub it all over the meat of the lobsters. Place them on a baking sheet, cut side up, and refrigerate.

Heat the broiler. Cut the zucchini into ¼-inch-thick rounds. Heat the olive oil in a large skillet over medium-high heat. Add the zucchini, season with salt and pepper, and sauté for 5 minutes, or until nicely browned but still crisp. Keep warm.

Broil the lobsters at least 8 inches below the broiling unit for 6 to 10 minutes, until the meat is tender and golden. (Little bits of white collagen will appear on the edges of the meat, indicating doneness.)

Arrange the lobsters on a platter, surround them with the zucchini, and serve.

LOBSTER THERMIDOR

4 servings

Years ago, as a cook at Domaine Chandon, Moët's California winery, I prepared a special banquet for the top people in the company. Philippe Jeanty, the twenty-year-old sous-chef, and I had made, among other dishes, lobster bisque. On the appointed day, the head chefs from Paul Bocuse and Roger Vergé strode into the kitchen and elbowed us aside. To our chagrin, they whipped up about five dozen egg yolks with cream and proceeded to "fatten" our lovely bisque. What had been special and French-Californian became leaden. Since that day, I've vowed to err on the side of light and tasty.

The base of a traditional lobster thermidor is an egg custard with cognac, wine, mustard, and butter (sometimes with Parmesan cheese added). Quite similar, in fact, to the bisque that the tradition-bound French made. I wanted an ethereal version of lobster thermidor. Here it is.

2 1¼-pound lobsters (if you can get them, live Catalina lobsters or other spiny lobsters also work well)	4 tablespoons (½ stick) unsalted butter
	1 tablespoon Dijon mustard
	2 tablespoons cognac
4 shallots	2 tablespoons minced fresh chives
2 garlic cloves	Kosher salt and freshly ground
1 pint cherry tomatoes	black pepper
1 cup dry white wine	3 tablespoons freshly grated
1 cup heavy cream	Parmesan cheese

Bring a large pot of salted water to a boil. Plunge the lobsters in and cook for 7 minutes. Remove and let cool.

Remove all the meat from the lobsters and cut into small dice. Dice the shallots. Mince the garlic. Halve the tomatoes.

In a medium saucepan, combine the shallots, garlic, and wine, bring to a boil over medium heat, and cook until the liquid is syrupy, about 10 minutes.

Add the cream and cook to reduce slightly, stirring occasionally. Add the lobster. Heat for 2 minutes, then swirl in the butter. Stir in the tomatoes, mustard, cognac, and chives. Season with salt and pepper.

Heat the broiler. Divide the mixture evenly among four heatproof bowls. Sprinkle with the Parmesan and broil, watching carefully, for 6 to 10 minutes, or until golden brown and bubbly. Serve.

SOFT-SHELL CRABS WITH SPICY PEAS

4 servings

Peas are at their best at the same time that soft-shell crabs begin to come into the market. You can make this dish in about 10 minutes. The peas cook together with the crabs and provide a delicious undertone that you'll find quite harmonious.

Have your fishmonger clean the crabs or do it yourself following the instructions on page 102. If you buy them cleaned, use them as soon as possible.

4 large soft-shell crabs, live and lively

2 pounds fresh peas in the shells,
     or 1½ cups frozen peas, thawed

1 lemon

4 tablespoons (½ stick) unsalted butter

1 teaspoon red pepper flakes
   Sea salt

Clean the crabs if necessary. Pat the crabs dry with paper towels. If using fresh peas, shuck them. Juice the lemon.

Melt 2 tablespoons of the butter in a large skillet over medium-high heat. When the butter stops foaming, add the crabs, top side down, and sauté for 3 minutes. The fat inside the crabs will crackle and pop. Flip the crabs and add the peas, pepper flakes, and sea salt to taste. Cook for 3 minutes longer, then remove the crabs to a platter and keep warm.

Turn off the heat, swirl in the remaining 2 tablespoons butter, and add lemon juice to taste. Season with salt if necessary.

Spoon the sauce and peas over the crabs and serve.

CRAB CAKES WITH RED CABBAGE SLAW

6 servings

If I had been diligent about writing down all my restaurant meals over the years, I'm sure I would have recorded a spell during which every tasting menu served me contained crab cakes, crab salad, or crab bisque. One such meal stands out. My dear friend Patrick Clark, who cooked last at the Tavern on the Green before passing away at a too-young age, cooked a mean-ass cake! He was a man of huge humor and size but delicate sensibilities. These crab cakes are a homage to him and his gentle ways.

Mayonnaise

1 lemon
1 cup corn oil or peanut oil
¼ cup olive oil
3 large egg yolks
Tabasco sauce

1 jalapeño or serrano chile
1½ pounds lump crabmeat

1 cup fresh bread crumbs
Kosher salt and freshly ground
black pepper
2 large egg yolks
1 small onion
4 ears corn
1 small head red cabbage
1 lemon
1 cup chopped mixed fresh herbs
(flat-leaf parsley, chives, and basil)
3 tablespoons olive oil
2 tablespoons unsalted butter

MAKE THE MAYONNAISE

Juice the lemon. Pour the corn or peanut oil and the olive oil into a measuring cup or a pitcher with a narrow spout. In a medium bowl, whisk the egg yolks and lemon juice together, then whisk for 3 minutes. Dribble in a few teaspoons of the oil mixture until the sauce begins to emulsify. Still whisking, drizzle in the rest of the oil in a very thin stream—not too fast, or the mayonnaise will "break," or curdle. The

mayonnaise should be quite stiff. Season to taste with Tabasco.

Cut the chile pepper in half. Discard the stem and seeds. Chop half of the chile into a small dice and cut the other half into julienne strips. Pick over the lump crabmeat for shells and cartilage and place the crabmeat in a bowl.

Add ½ cup of the bread crumbs, the diced chile, and half the mayonnaise to the crabmeat and mix lightly just until incorporated. The mixture should remain light, but you should be able to form it into cakes. Season with salt and pepper. Divide the mixture into 6 portions and form cakes that are about 1 inch thick.

In a shallow bowl, whisk the egg yolks with 3 tablespoons water. Spread the remaining ½ cup bread crumbs on a plate. Dip the crab cakes in the egg yolk mixture, turning to coat, then coat them in the bread crumbs. Place them on a plastic-wrap-lined tray and refrigerate for 30 minutes before cooking to firm them up.

Thinly slice the onion. Husk the corn and cut the kernels off the cobs with a sharp knife.

Julienne the red cabbage. Juice the lemon. Toss the cabbage in a bowl with the mixed herbs, julienned chile pepper, and 2 tablespoons of the

mayonnaise. Add the lemon juice and salt and pepper to taste, along with 1 tablespoon of the olive oil. Toss well and set aside.

Heat a large cast-iron skillet over medium heat. Add 1 tablespoon of the olive oil and the butter and heat until hot. Fry the crab cakes, 3 at a time, turning once, until golden brown on both sides. Transfer to a platter and keep warm. Fry the remaining crab cakes, using the remaining 1 tablespoon olive oil.

Add the onion and corn to the pan, and sauté just until tender. Add to the cabbage slaw and toss.

Divide the slaw among serving plates. Place the crab cakes on top and serve with the remaining mayonnaise.

IN MY HEART OF HEARTS,
I WOULD BE VERY HAPPY ON
A VEGETARIAN DIET.

VEGETABLES

In my heart of hearts, I would be very happy on a vegetarian diet. When you are slaving over a hot stove, the idea of eating anything simply fades. You've probably noticed that when you cook, you tend to eat less at the table—sometimes a *lot* less. One thing that appeals to me after a long evening working the grill is a little ragout of vegetables or a simple pasta with tomatoes, basil, and grated Grana cheese. On my day off, my lunch is generally a chopped salad made with the freshest market vegetables and garlic croutons. Only on holiday do I indulge like a regular person, when there is no workaholic guilt to suppress my appetite.

Most of the vegetable dishes here can be expanded to make main courses or served as appetizers or lunch dishes. A great vegetarian recipe relies on the intrinsic strengths of well-sourced vegetables. An eggplant that is shiny and firm to the touch has much more flavor than an old, tired, wrinkly one. Similarly, tomatoes are at their best when they have just been picked that morning. It's thrilling to snatch a chile or a sprig of tarragon from your garden in the midmorning sun. The fresher your vegetables, the more they will infuse dishes with that wonderful essence of soil-bound flavor.

The vision of my own little organic garden finally came to reality a couple of years ago. Nothing is more satisfying than cooking what you've sown. The breadth of the yield from just a small plot is nothing short of astounding. Not until you've picked your own zucchini blossoms and cherry tomatoes does the notion of "fresh" really come into play. It is probably true that the best cooks are those who have become or want to become good gardeners.

As for my final meal, I want a potato. That's it, with a bottle of Bollinger RD champagne 1975. What kind of potato? A roasted Idaho stuffed with sour cream, chives, butter, and bacon. Or a bowl of new potatoes with loads of caviar and melted butter. Or mashed potatoes with enough cream and butter to enrage my cardiologist. Too many potatoes are barely enough.

VEGETABLES

JW FRIES

6 to 8 servings

Every potato aficionado has a theory about which ones are best for French fries. Any very firm, large organic russet potato originating in the northwestern states— Idaho, Washington, or Oregon—will produce a fabulous French fry. If you can find potatoes from the Klamath Basin in Oregon, use them. I also like Yukon Gold potatoes, but they need to be large. The rest is science. The key is to soak the fries in ice water to remove all their surface starch, then fry them first at a low temperature, taking care to prevent them from taking on any color, chill them, and then fry again to brown and crisp them. A pain, yes, but well worth it to achieve the ultimate French fries!

6–8 large russet potatoes (about 8 pounds), preferably organic

6–8 cups peanut oil or corn oil (fresh or used once before to fry potatoes)

Sea salt

Peel the potatoes and place them in a bowl of ice water. Refrigerate for at least 8 hours, or overnight.

Using a sharp knife, cut each potato lengthwise into 3 slices. Cut each slice lengthwise into fifths, yielding fries that are approximately ½ inch wide. Place them in a bowl of cold water.

Heat the oil in a 10-quart heavy pot over high heat until the oil reaches 250 degrees. Meanwhile, drain the potatoes well and pat dry thoroughly with a kitchen towel.

You are going to fry the potatoes twice. Add them to the hot oil in batches—do not crowd— and blanch for 5 minutes. Carefully remove the potatoes and let them drain and cool on paper towels. Spread the potatoes on a baking sheet and refrigerate, uncovered, for at least 1 hour, or up to 6 hours. Set the pot of oil aside.

Bring the French fries to room temperature, about 30 minutes.

Heat the oil to 300 degrees. Fry the potatoes, again in batches, until crisp and golden brown— not pale gold and not brown! Drain on a brown paper bag or paper towels, sprinkle with salt, and serve quickly, before they cool.

BRAISED CARROTS WITH SAFFRON

4 to 6 servings

A few years ago, I followed the path of Don Quixote and Sancho Panza through La Mancha. The heart of Spain produces the most amazing (and expensive) spice in the world, saffron, the hand-harvested yellow-orange stigmas of a crocus flower. While other parts of Spain, as well as Italy, Greece, Pakistan, and India, all produce saffron, in La Mancha they rightly claim the title of the world's finest.

As we watched, four women worked intently over a table covered with lavender crocuses. The odor was intoxicating. To get one kilo of saffron, workers must pick the stigmas from 250,000 blossoms.

Inspired by my trip, I made these carrots, which are glazed in butter, sherry vinegar, and saffron. Be sure the saffron is fresh, and don't use too little—or too much. And don't add it too soon, or it will dominate the carrots.

2   pounds medium carrots, preferably a
    mixture of orange and yellow
    Sea salt
¼   cup olive oil

A good pinch of saffron threads
2   tablespoons sherry vinegar
2   tablespoons unsalted butter
    Freshly ground black pepper

Trim and peel the carrots if you like, but leave them whole. Place them in a medium saucepan with 1½ cups water and a little sea salt and bring to a boil. Cover and boil gently over medium heat until the carrots are al dente, about 15 minutes. Drain the carrots and pat them dry.

Heat the olive oil in a large skillet over medium-low heat. When it's warm, add the carrots and cook gently for 3 minutes. Add the saffron and sherry vinegar and cook for 2 minutes, turning the carrots once or twice. Add the butter, cover the skillet, and let stand off the heat for 5 minutes.

Season the carrots with salt and pepper and serve.

RESTAURANT-STYLE VEGETABLES

8 servings

When my restaurant Jams opened, I served a ragout of seven to ten colorful, flavorful vegetables that changed nightly as the accompaniment to a majority of the main courses. The vegetables proved a great hit, and in ensuing years I have served them as a vegetarian alternative to the fish, meat, and poultry entrées.

The combinations of vegetables need to meld harmoniously, and they should retain a bit of crunch.

12 radishes	6 broccoli florets
½ pound yellow wax beans	4 tablespoons (½ stick) unsalted butter
1 red bell pepper	Kosher salt and freshly ground black
1 green bell pepper	pepper
1 medium zucchini	½ pint cherry or pear tomatoes
1 medium yellow summer squash	½ cup chopped mixed fresh herbs, such
8 new potatoes or small Yukon	as tarragon, basil, rosemary, sage,
Gold potatoes	oregano, and/or chervil
6 cauliflower florets	

Trim the radishes. Leave them whole if they're small, or halve or quarter them if large. Top and tail the wax beans. Stem and seed the peppers and cut them into bite-sized squares. Quarter the zucchini and yellow squash and cut into wedges, or slice diagonally. Leave the skins on the new potatoes or peel the Yukon Golds.

Bring two large saucepans of salted water to a boil. Add the potatoes to one pan and cook for 15 minutes. Add the radishes and cook for 5 minutes more, until both are tender. Drain well.

Add the wax beans to the other saucepan and cook just until tender, 5 to 8 minutes. Remove

them with a mesh strainer or slotted spoon. Add the cauliflower and cook until tender, 5 to 8 minutes. Remove and cook the broccoli, 5 to 8 minutes; remove the broccoli from the pan.

Melt the butter in a large skillet over medium heat. Add the peppers and squashes and cook for 5 minutes. Season with salt and pepper and add the blanched vegetables. Cook for 5 minutes more, or until all the vegetables are tender.

Check the seasoning, stir in the tomatoes and herbs, and heat briefly to warm the tomatoes. Serve.

LATE-AUTUMN VEGETABLE CASSEROLE

6 to 8 hearty side-dish servings or 4 to 6 main-dish servings

This vegetarian casserole will satisfy anybody. I love the rich sweetness of the Hubbard squash with the mushrooms and root vegetables. Serve it in sturdy bowls, with a subtle Pinot Noir. The casserole tastes even better reheated the next day. You can serve it as a side dish to any roasted meat or poultry, toss it with pasta to feed a larger group, or serve it with corn bread and Zinfandel as a fireside meal. You can also vary the vegetables a bit—feel free to improvise if celery root is not available: try parsnips, rutabaga, and/or beets.

3 pounds Hubbard or butternut squash
3 tablespoons olive oil, plus additional
    for rubbing the squash
Kosher salt and freshly ground
    black pepper
1 pound white button mushrooms
2 medium onions
6 garlic cloves
4 large leeks

2 small celery roots
1 cup assorted fresh herb leaves, such
    as sage, flat-leaf parsley, rosemary,
    chives, and basil
3 drained canned plum tomatoes,
    preferably San Marzano
1 cup fresh bread crumbs
½ cup freshly grated Parmesan cheese

Heat the oven to 325 degrees.

Split the squash lengthwise in half and remove the strings and seeds. Rub the flesh with a bit of olive oil and season with salt and pepper. Place the squash on a baking sheet and roast for 45 minutes to 1 hour, until tender. Set aside to cool slightly. Reduce the oven temperature to 400 degrees.

Meanwhile, clean and chop the mushrooms. Chop the onions. Smash the garlic. Trim the leeks, split lengthwise, and wash them well, then chop. Peel and chop the celery root. Chop the tomatoes. Chop the herbs.

Heat the 3 tablespoons olive oil in a large enameled cast-iron casserole or Dutch oven over medium heat. Add the onions, garlic, leeks, and celery root and cook, stirring, for 10 minutes, or until tender. Add the mushrooms and cook for 5 minutes. Scoop out the squash in tablespoon-sized chunks and add to the casserole. Add the tomatoes and herbs and season with salt and pepper.

Sprinkle with the bread crumbs and cheese. Bake for 20 minutes, or until deep golden brown on top and bubbly. Serve.

MIXED PEPPERS AND ONIONS

4 to 6 servings

The best peppers come in late summer, when they are large, dusky, heavy, and bursting with ripe, sweet flavors. Small peppers will not have good flavor.

8   assorted bell peppers (brown, green, purple, and/or red with streaks of black—try them all!)
¼   cup plus 2 tablespoons olive oil
    Kosher salt and freshly ground black pepper

2   sweet onions, such as Vidalia
2   garlic cloves
1   jalapeño chile

Heat the oven to 400 degrees.

Stem the peppers, cut into quarters, and seed them. Place them on a rimmed baking sheet. Sprinkle with 2 tablespoons of the olive oil and ¼ cup water. Season with salt and pepper and roast for 30 minutes, or until tender.

Meanwhile, dice the onions. Smash the garlic cloves. Halve, seed, and mince the jalapeño.

Heat the remaining ¼ cup olive oil in a large heavy skillet over medium heat. Add the onions, garlic, and jalapeño and cook, stirring, for 10 minutes, or until tender. Remove from the heat.

Place the bell peppers in a bowl, add the jalapeño-onion mixture, and toss well. Season and serve warm or at room temperature.

SUCCOTASH

8 side-dish servings or 4 main-dish servings

This spectacular stew can be the centerpiece of a great late-summer dinner. The vegetables are transformed by the slow braising, which develops and intensifies their flavors. Even more magic happens if you let the stew sit overnight. The only thing *not* to do is to cook the vegetables until they fall apart.

6 ears corn	2 pounds lima or butter beans in the shell
6 garlic cloves	or 12 ounces frozen thawed
1 cup loosely packed fresh basil leaves (reserve the stems for the broth)	3 sweet onions, such as Vidalia
Kosher salt	4 large ripe tomatoes
¾ pound green beans	2 tablespoons olive oil
¾ pound yellow wax beans	4 tablespoons (½ stick) unsalted butter
1 pound fresh cranberry beans in the shell (½ pound shelled; optional)	Freshly ground black pepper

Husk the corn and cut the kernels from the cobs, reserving the cobs. Set the corn kernels aside. Cut the cobs into quarters.

MAKE THE VEGETABLE BROTH
Combine the corncobs, 2 of the garlic cloves, the basil stems, and 4 cups water in a large saucepan. Add salt to taste and bring to a simmer. Simmer over low heat for 30 minutes. Strain the broth into another large saucepan and bring to a boil.

Meanwhile, top and tail the green and wax beans. Shell the cranberry beans, if using, and the limas or butter beans. Dice the onions. Core and dice the tomatoes. Smash the remaining 4 garlic cloves.

When the broth is boiling, add the green and wax beans and cook just until al dente. Remove with a mesh strainer or slotted spoon and set aside. Add the cranberry beans and cook just until tender, 10 to 15 minutes. Remove and let cool. Add the limas and cook until tender, 5 to 10 minutes. Remove and let cool.

Heat the olive oil and butter in a large enameled cast-iron casserole or Dutch oven over medium heat. Add the corn, onions, garlic, and salt to taste and cook for 10 minutes, stirring occasionally. Add all the beans and cook for 10 minutes.

Add the tomatoes and basil and cook for 3 to 5 minutes. Adjust the seasonings with salt and pepper and serve. (The succotash can be covered and refrigerated for up to 3 days.)

ROASTED CORN WITH RED PEPPER BUTTER

3 to 6 servings

One of the most talented, intelligent, and well-organized chefs I ever worked with was Helen Chardack, who has since left the restaurant business to raise two wonderful daughters with her husband, chef Alfred Portale. One warm day, Helen was examining the summer's first batch of delicious Long Island corn. Knowing that I liked the idea of red pepper butter with corn, she quickly grilled the ears whole over a mesquite fire. Then, when the corn was done, she pulled back the charred husks, discarding the black ones, and rubbed the hot kernels with red pepper butter.

6   ears corn
1   jalapeño chile
1   red bell pepper
8   tablespoons (1 stick) unsalted butter,
     at room temperature

1   garlic clove
1   teaspoon sea salt

Prepare a medium-hot fire in a grill.

Pull back the corn husk from each ear of corn, leaving it attached at the base of the cob, and remove the silk. Pull the husk back up around the corn.

Grill the jalapeño and red pepper over medium-hot coals, turning occasionally, until blackened and blistered all over. Place them in a bowl, cover with plastic wrap, and let steam for 15 minutes.

Peel the peppers with your fingers (do not rinse), stem, and seed them. Transfer to a blender, add the butter, garlic, and sea salt, and puree until the butter is red and homogenous.

Grill the corn over medium-low heat until it's tender, rolling the corn frequently, about 12 minutes. Using kitchen mitts, pull back the husk and place the ears on a platter. Slather with the red pepper butter and serve hot.

STEAMED ARTICHOKES WITH GARLIC MAYONNAISE

4 servings

Choose the freshest, biggest artichokes you can find, with the sharpest spikes on their leaves. The varieties without spikes are not as flavorful. Lift them one by one to make sure they feel heavy in your hand and are hard and squeaky when you squeeze them. If people look at you in the store as if you're mad, don't worry—as soon as you leave the area, they will do the same!

4 **large artichokes**	1 **cup olive oil**
	3 **large egg yolks**
Mayonnaise	**Sea salt**
1 **lemon**	1 **garlic clove**
4 **fresh flat-leaf parsley sprigs**	

Fit a steamer basket or a bamboo steamer into a large pot filled with a few inches of water. Rinse the artichokes, trim the stems if necessary, and place them in the steamer, stem end down. Cover and bring the water to a boil, then reduce the heat slightly and steam the artichokes until tender, 30 to 40 minutes. The artichokes are fully cooked when a leaf from the second layer of outer leaves pulls out easily.

MEANWHILE, MAKE THE MAYONNAISE

Juice the lemon and put the juice in a medium bowl. Strip the leaves from the parsley, chop them, and add them to the bowl. Pour the oil into a pitcher with a narrow spout. Add the egg yolks and ½ teaspoon salt to the bowl with the lemon juice and whisk to blend, then whisk for 3 minutes. Whisking briskly, dribble in a few teaspoons of olive oil until the sauce begins to emulsify. Still whisking, slowly drizzle in the rest of the oil in a very thin stream—not too fast, or the mayonnaise will "break," or curdle. Mince the garlic. Stir it into the mayonnaise and season with salt to taste. You may need to adjust the consistency by whisking in a little hot water; the mayo should be light and fluffy. Cover and refrigerate until ready to serve.

Serve the artichokes hot, warm, at room temperature, or cold, with the mayonnaise for dipping.

ZUCCHINI BLOSSOM BEIGNETS
WITH SUN-DRIED-TOMATO MAYONNAISE

4 servings

My adventures in my grandparents' garden did not include horticultural instructions about the propagation of squash plants. Then one day a purveyor arrived at my restaurant with a flat of perfect zucchini blossoms. I proceeded to try roasting, sautéing, and deep-frying them. Deep-frying is the way to go, and the slightly anise flavor of the blossoms and their delicate texture hold up well to a tempura-type beer batter. I like to serve them with a sun-dried-tomato mayonnaise. If you feel so inclined, you can stuff the blossoms with some finely minced zucchini with a few herbs and olive oil or a little chopped tomato mixed with a good soft goat cheese.

Zucchini flowers are delicate and will wilt if left around too long. Prepare them soon after you pick them. Do watch out for any moving creatures—inspect the blossoms carefully before you fry.

Mayonnaise

¼   **cup sun-dried tomatoes (not packed in oil)**

1   **lemon**

1½   **cups corn oil or peanut oil**

4   **large egg yolks**

   Balsamic vinegar

1   **teaspoon finely chopped fresh tarragon**

   Kosher salt and freshly ground black pepper

Batter

½   **cup all-purpose flour**

2   **large eggs**

½   **cup lager, or as needed**

2   **tablespoons olive oil**

   Kosher salt and freshly ground black pepper

8   **large zucchini or other squash blossoms**

   About 4 cups corn oil or peanut oil, for deep-frying

Soak the sun-dried tomatoes in hot water until softened, about 30 minutes.

MEANWHILE, MAKE THE BATTER
Put the flour in a large bowl and make a well in the middle of the mound. Separate the eggs and add the yolks to the well. Put the whites in a medium bowl, cover, and refrigerate. Pour the beer into the yolks. Add the olive oil and salt and pepper to taste. Beat until well blended, adding a little more beer if necessary to make a light, fluffy batter. Let the batter rest for 30 minutes.

MAKE THE MAYONNAISE

Juice the lemon. Pour the oil into a measuring cup or a pitcher with a narrow spout. Drain the tomatoes and process in a food processor to a chunky puree. Add the egg yolks, ½ teaspoon vinegar, and lemon juice and pulse. Then pulse while drizzling in the oil in a very thin stream—not too fast, or the mayonnaise will "break," or curdle. When the mayonnaise is just thick but not stiff, transfer it to a small bowl and add the tarragon and a few more drops of balsamic vinegar. Season with salt if necessary and pepper to taste (some sun-dried tomatoes are saltier than others). Cover and refrigerate.

PREPARE THE ZUCCHINI BLOSSOMS

Carefully open up the zucchini blossoms and remove the stamens. Close up the flowers and refrigerate, covered with a damp paper towel, until you're ready to fry.

Beat the egg whites with an electric mixer until soft peaks form, then fold them into the batter.

Heat the oil in a large deep pot to 350 degrees. Fry about 4 blossoms at a time; do not crowd the pot. Dredge the blossoms in the batter, in batches, and use long tongs to lower the flowers into the hot oil, holding them by the stems. When they are nicely browned, remove with a slotted spoon and drain on paper towels.

Serve with the sun-dried-tomato mayonnaise. The blossoms can be served at room temperature, but they are at their best when hot.

BROILED EGGPLANT

4 to 8 servings

A sweet, vine-ripened eggplant picked yesterday, from the farmers' market or your own garden, will trump a supermarket variety hands down. Store-bought eggplants can be fresh and sweet, but you need to know how to choose them. Look for very firm flesh and smooth skin. Baby eggplants are cute but have no flavor. For this recipe, I use 8- to 10-inch lavender or purple eggplants. If you can get white ones, they are a bit sweeter. But freshness is the most important thing.

Some recipes call for eggplant slices to be salted liberally, then wiped clean and patted dry. This step isn't necessary.

A cooked eggplant will "puff" when it's done, as steam is released by the eggplant.

8   **medium eggplants**
¼   **cup olive oil, plus extra for drizzling**

**Kosher salt and freshly ground
   black pepper**
2   **tablespoons freshly grated Parmesan
   cheese**

Heat the broiler.

Cut off the stem ends of the eggplants and split them lengthwise in half.

Place the eggplants in a large bowl and add the olive oil and salt and pepper to taste. Place the eggplants cut side down on two rimmed baking sheets. Broil, one sheet at a time, 5 inches from the broiling unit for 3 to 4 minutes, until golden. Turn and cook until they puff, 2 to 5 minutes.

When they have puffed, arrange them cut side up on a platter. Sprinkle with olive oil, pepper, and the grated Parmesan and serve.

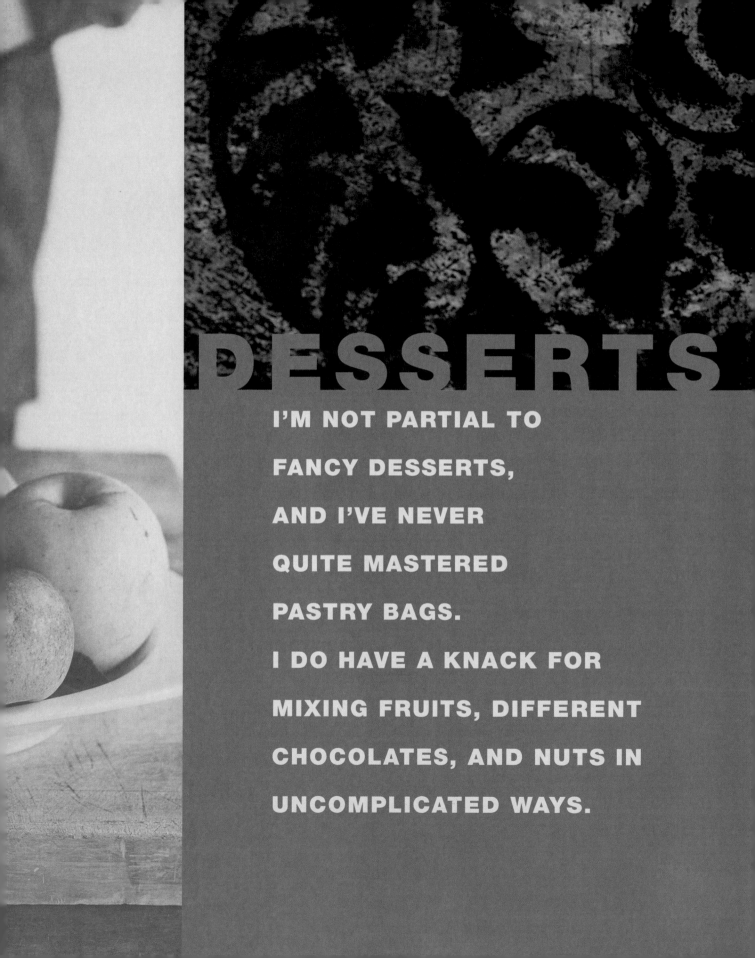

DESSERTS

I'M NOT PARTIAL TO
FANCY DESSERTS,
AND I'VE NEVER
QUITE MASTERED
PASTRY BAGS.
I DO HAVE A KNACK FOR
MIXING FRUITS, DIFFERENT
CHOCOLATES, AND NUTS IN
UNCOMPLICATED WAYS.

My friends know me as a closet cookie monster. My kids know all too well that they have to hide their Halloween candy. And God forbid that we receive a box of very expensive chocolates from Wittamer in Brussels.

I'm not partial to fancy desserts, and I've never quite mastered pastry bags. I do have a knack for mixing fruits, different chocolates, and nuts in uncomplicated ways. The desserts in this chapter are straightforward, but with little twists to make them interesting. The ingredients are mostly American, the techniques European.

In terms of ingredients, heavy cream should be a kitchen standard. The butter you use should be fresh and unsalted. I also recommend keeping a few pints of premium ice cream around, to dress up any dessert. Other items that you should keep on hand include whole nutmeg (which keeps forever), cinnamon sticks, cloves, and if possible, vanilla beans. The last are magical, fragrant, and exotic, and after they've been used, they can be recycled to flavor a bowl of sugar.

Your equipment need not be extravagant. I do recommend a good food processor and a handheld electric mixer or a strong stationary one. I like using a heavy rolling pin—the heavier the better. Great whisks are a necessity. I use a balloon whip (not the wimpy grocery-store variety) and a long pastry whip. Pastry scrapers and heatproof rubber spatulas are also important. I like heavy ceramic mixing bowls. Your baking pans should be heavy, too. Cooling racks for cakes, cookies, and pies are essential. Parchment paper is a good thing.

Read the recipes completely before you start. You can
vary some of the ingredients according to your own
tastes, but don't fool around with the basics.

Try to complete the dessert portion of your meal when
your kitchen is quiet and relatively free of
distractions. Remember that heat and cold and
humidity are all factors in getting a pastry recipe to
perform correctly.

DESSERTS

APRICOT-MANGO CRISP

6 to 8 servings

This crisp has been a perennial winner at all my restaurants. Perhaps that's because of its homey, rustic flavors or perhaps it's because it reminds everyone of childhood. Crisps are a snap to prepare, and you can use practically any fruit or combination of fruits—whatever's in season. In fact, the only fruits that are not appropriate are the members of the citrus family, which just disintegrate into mushiness.

1 cup walnuts	½ teaspoon ground cloves
¾ cup unblanched almonds	2 ripe but not soft mangoes
½ cup all-purpose flour	2 pounds apricots
1 cup sugar	10 tablespoons (1 stick plus 2 tablespoons)
Pinch of salt	cold unsalted butter
½ teaspoon freshly grated nutmeg	Vanilla ice cream, for serving (optional)
½ teaspoon ground cinnamon	

Heat the oven to 425 degrees. Butter a 9-inch square or an 11-x-7-inch rectangular baking dish.

Finely chop the nuts and place in a medium bowl. Add the flour, sugar, salt, nutmeg, cinnamon, and cloves and mix well.

Peel the mangoes, cut the flesh from the pits, and cube it. Peel and pit the apricots and cut them into bite-sized slices. Combine the fruits in a bowl and toss together with 1 tablespoon of the flour mixture. Let sit for 5 minutes.

Cut the butter into 1-inch cubes. Using your fingertips or a pastry blender, work the butter into the remaining dry mixture until it is the size of peas.

Transfer the fruit to the baking dish. Press down lightly to make an even layer, then cover the fruit with the butter-flour mixture.

Bake for 30 minutes, or until the apricots are tender and the top is browned. Serve hot or warm, with a scoop of ice cream if you like.

VARIATION: APPLE-PEAR CRISP

Substitute 3 apples such as Jonagold and 5 Bosc pears, peeled, cored, and cut into cubes, for the apricots and mangoes.

GINGERBREAD WITH BRANDIED PLUMS

8 to 10 servings

Everyone loves gingerbread. I wanted to add some unusual flavor to my ginger-bread, without taking away its most beloved qualities. Fresh ginger has a spiciness and zip that the powdered form doesn't. Almond extract adds another pleasant di-mension without detracting from the ginger.

Gingerbread

1¼	cups walnuts
⅔	cup macadamia nuts
8	tablespoons (1 stick) unsalted butter
2½	cups all-purpose flour
1½	teaspoons baking soda
½	teaspoon salt
1	teaspoon ground cinnamon
1	teaspoon freshly grated nutmeg
1	teaspoon ground cloves
2	large eggs
½	cup sugar
¼	cup grated peeled fresh ginger

½	cup molasses
½	cup honey
2	tablespoons dark rum
2	teaspoons almond extract

Plums

½	pound plums
2	tablespoons unsalted butter
2	tablespoons sugar
½	cup grappa
1	cup well-chilled heavy cream
	A splash of dark rum

MAKE THE GINGERBREAD

Heat the oven to 375 degrees. Butter a 9-x-5-x-3-inch loaf pan and dust it with flour.

Spread the nuts on a rimmed baking sheet and toast in the oven for about 8 minutes, stirring once or twice, until fragrant. Let cool, then coarsely chop.

Melt the butter. Let cool slightly.

Sift the flour with the baking soda, salt, cinnamon, nutmeg, and cloves; set aside.

In a large bowl, using an electric mixer, beat the eggs with the sugar until blended. Slowly beat in the melted butter. Add the grated ginger, then the molasses, honey, rum, almond extract, and 1 cup water, beating until well blended. On low speed, gradually add the flour mixture, beating just until incorporated. Fold in the nuts.

Pour the batter into the prepared pan. Bake for 45 minutes, or until a skewer inserted in the center comes out clean.

Halve, pit, and slice the plums. Place them in a medium saucepan with the butter, sugar, and grappa and bring to a simmer. Simmer for 10 minutes, stirring occasionally. Remove from the heat and set aside to cool to room temperature.

In a medium bowl, beat the cream with rum to taste until soft peaks form. Cover and refrigerate.

When the gingerbread is done, cool it in the pan on a wire rack for 10 minutes, then remove it from the loaf pan and let cool to warm on the rack.

Slice it into 1-inch slices and garnish with the plum mixture and whipped cream.

PEARS POACHED IN BEAUJOLAIS

4 servings

The simplicity of poached fruit has always appealed to me. The only problem is keeping it from tasting as if it were meant for a high school cafeteria.

The classic recipe for poached pears involves a poaching liquid of sugar syrup flavored with wine, but I think the Beaujolais has enough sugar and fruitiness on its own. I interject a bit of spice and a little heat, along with some tartness, by introducing black peppercorns, cinnamon, and orange liqueur.

Serve with a shortbread cookie, if you like.

4 large ripe Bosc pears
2 cups good Beaujolais
¼ cup Grand Marnier or Cointreau

1 teaspoon whole black peppercorns
1 cinnamon stick

Peel the pears and core them. Place them in a saucepan that holds them tightly. Add the Beaujolais, liqueur, peppercorns, and cinnamon stick. Bring to a simmer, then poach the pears gently over medium-low heat until they're just tender, about 20 minutes.

Let the pears cool in the poaching liquid.

Transfer the pears to four bowls. Strain the poaching liquid over them and serve hot, room temperature, or chilled.

TARTE TATIN

6 to 8 servings

This is hands-down the most popular of all of my apple desserts. I developed it after many hours of struggling to make a tart that wasn't too sweet or too heavy. The apples are cooked briefly in a caramel-butter sauce, then covered with puff pastry and baked. Once baked, the tart is inverted to show off the apples in their decorative pattern. Serve warm or at room temperature.

8–10 Jonagold or Fuji apples
½ cup sugar
4 tablespoons (½ stick) unsalted butter

Quick Puff Pastry (page 271)
1 cup crème fraîche or vanilla ice cream, for serving

Trace the circumference of the top of a 12-inch cast-iron skillet onto a piece of parchment paper so that you will know what size your pastry should be; set aside.

Peel and core the apples, then cut them in half from the stem to the blossom end. Trim the bottoms so the apples can stand on end. Combine the sugar and butter in the skillet and cook, stirring, over medium heat until the sugar dissolves. Then continue to cook until the mixture is lightly caramel colored.

Add the apples, lining them up like soldiers in a circle around the perimeter of the pan, then making a smaller circle within that one. Fill in the center with apples if necessary. If there are any extras, pile them on top. Cook for 10 minutes. Remove from the heat and let cool.

Meanwhile, roll out the puff pastry ¼ inch thick. Using the parchment paper as a guide, cut a round of pastry to fit over the apples with a bit of overlap. Prick the pastry all over with a fork, place on a baking sheet, and refrigerate for 15 minutes.

Heat the oven to 400 degrees.

Set the pastry over the apples in the skillet. Place the skillet on a baking sheet, transfer to the oven, and bake for 30 minutes, or until the pastry is a deep golden brown.

Remove the tart from the oven. Place a heavy round platter at least 2 inches larger than the skillet over the skillet and, using oven mitts, quickly but carefully invert the plate and the skillet. Let it sit for 5 minutes, then lift the skillet off. Rearrange the apples if necessary, replacing any that may have stuck to the skillet. Serve with the crème fraîche.

MY PASTRY CRUST

Makes enough for two 10-inch crusts

The more-than-usual amount of water in this dough prevents the buildup of gluten (the enemy of flakiness) and produces a distinctively moist, tender, soft dough. In addition to keeping the dough flaky, the extra moisture makes for a crumbly texture that everyone loves.

This recipe makes enough dough for 2 crusts; if you need just one, freeze the extra wrapped in plastic.

6   cups all-purpose flour
⅓   cup sugar
1   tablespoon salt

½   pound (2 sticks) cold unsalted butter, cut into small cubes
1   cup ice water

In a large bowl, whisk together the flour, sugar, and salt. Make a well in the middle and add the butter and water. Lightly and quickly work in the butter with your fingertips, until it is in pea-sized pieces and the dough comes together; it will be soft and moist.

Divide the dough in half. Form each half into a disk, wrap in plastic, and refrigerate for at least 1 hour before rolling it out. (The dough can be refrigerated for up to 2 days or frozen for up to 2 months.)

LEMON-LIME MERINGUE PIE

6 to 8 servings

This variation on the famous Key lime pie of Florida is a lemon-lime-curd-filled pie with a mountain-high meringue topping. It's made with a combination of ordinary lime and lemon juice, but if Key limes and/or Meyer lemons are available, by all means use them. The filling is a rich mixture of egg yolks and citrus juice, with a little cornstarch to bind it. The trick is to make it as light as possible.

The pie should be served the day it's made, or the meringue will weep.

½ recipe My Pastry Crust (page 266)
3 limes
3 lemons (Meyer if possible)
6 large eggs
2 tablespoons unsalted butter

2 cups sugar
3 tablespoons cornstarch
Pinch of salt
Confectioners' sugar, for dusting

On a lightly floured surface, roll out the dough to a 12-inch round. Fit it into a 9-inch pie pan and trim the excess dough. Refrigerate for 30 minutes.

Juice the limes. Grate the zest from the lemons, then juice the lemons as well.

Separate the eggs and place the yolks in a small bowl and the whites in a large bowl. Whisk the egg yolks and refrigerate the whites. Combine the butter, 1 cup of the sugar, and the cornstarch in a heavy medium saucepan and cook over low heat, whisking constantly, for 2 minutes. Whisk the yolks into the pan and cook, whisking constantly, for 5 minutes. Gradually whisk in the citrus juices, whisking constantly. When the mixture has thickened slightly, add the grated zest and cook until thickened. Transfer the

filling to a buttered bowl and cover with a piece of plastic wrap placed directly against the surface. Let cool.

Heat the oven to 375 degrees.

Prick the pie shell all over with a fork. Line it with aluminum foil and fill with dried beans, rice, or pie weights. Bake for 15 minutes. Remove the foil and weights and bake for 8 to 10 minutes longer, or until the crust is golden brown. Remove the crust from the oven and let cool on a rack.

Heat the broiler. Fill the cooled crust with the lemon-lime curd.

Using an electric mixer, beat the egg whites with the salt until fluffy. Gradually add the remaining cup of sugar, about 2 tablespoons at a time, and

continue to beat until stiff, shiny peaks form. Spread the meringue generously over the filling, making sure to cover completely and mounding the filling in the center. Use the back of a large spoon to make peaks of meringue.

Place the finished pie under the broiler at a distance of at least 5 inches from the broiling unit. Watch carefully! As soon as the peaks start turning golden, turn the pie as necessary for even coloring, but also to cook the meringue through. Let cool.

Just before serving, dust the pie with confectioners' sugar.

FLOURLESS CHOCOLATE ESPRESSO TART

8 to 10 servings

This sinfully rich cake is basically a fallen soufflé. It uses almond meal in place of flour to give the cake texture. You can make almond meal easily in your food processor: just pulse almonds until they're pulverized (do not overprocess, though, or you will get almond butter).

The quality of chocolate is of great importance. The brand that I've settled on as my standby is Valrhona, made in France. Lindt, Scharffen Berger, and Ghirardelli are also good.

½ recipe Quick Puff Pastry
    (recipe follows)
12 tablespoons (1½ sticks) unsalted
    butter
6 ounces bittersweet chocolate
3 large eggs
1½ cups sugar

¼ cup brewed espresso or very
    strong coffee
⅔ cup ground almonds
    Pinch of salt
1 tablespoon unsweetened cocoa powder
    (optional)
1 tablespoon confectioners' sugar
    (optional)

Heat the oven to 350 degrees.

Roll out the puff pastry to a 12-inch round about ½ inch thick and fit it into a 9-inch fluted tart pan with a removable bottom. Trim the excess dough. Prick the pastry all over with the tines of a fork. Butter a piece of aluminum foil and line the pastry with the foil, buttered side down. Fill with dried beans, rice, or pie weights. Bake the tart shell until light golden brown, about 25 minutes. Transfer the pastry to a wire rack. Remove the foil and pie weights. Leave the oven on.

Melt the butter and the chocolate in a large heatproof bowl set over a saucepan of simmering water, stirring until smooth. Remove from the heat.

Separate the eggs, placing the whites in a large bowl. Stir the yolks into the chocolate-butter mixture with a wooden spoon and mix well. Stir in the sugar. Add the espresso, then stir in the ground almonds.

Whip the egg whites with the salt until they are soft peaks. Fold one quarter of the whites into the chocolate mixture, then fold in the rest of the whites.

Pour the chocolate mixture into the puff pastry shell and bake for 25 to 30 minutes, or until a toothpick inserted in the middle comes out sticky. Let the tart cool on a wire rack for at least 45 minutes. The cake will fall as it cools. If you like, put the cocoa powder and confectioners' sugar in a sieve and dust the top of the tart. Serve.

QUICK PUFF PASTRY

Makes enough for two 9-inch crusts

½ pound (2 sticks) unsalted butter	Ice water
4 cups all-purpose flour, plus about ½ cup more for rolling out	1 tablespoon salt

Melt 4 tablespoons of the butter. Put the flour in a large bowl and make a well in the center. Add the melted butter, salt, and ¾ cup ice water to the well and mix gently to create a soft dough, adding a little more water if necessary. Chill in the freezer for 10 minutes.

Using a rolling pin, pound and mash the remaining 12 tablespoons butter into a 6-x-8-inch brick.

On a generously floured surface, roll out the dough to a 10-inch square. Place the block of butter in the center and wrap the dough around it to enclose the butter. Wrap in plastic and refrigerate for 1 hour.

Place the dough on a floured work surface, seam side down, and roll it out to a 10-x-15-inch rectangle. Fold the dough in thirds, like a business letter. Turn the dough so a short end is toward you and roll it out again to a 10-x-15-inch rectangle. Fold it in thirds again, wrap, and refrigerate for 1 hour.

Divide the dough in half. Wrap in plastic and refrigerate until ready to use. (The dough can be refrigerated overnight or frozen for up to 1 month.)

ANGEL FOOD CAKE WITH TOFFEE CRUNCH

8 servings

My absolute favorite dessert spot as a child was Blum's, the pastry emporium of San Francisco. It served a coffee-toffee cake that was so good it gave me goose bumps. I'm sorry to say that Blum's is gone and so is the recipe, but I have tried to resurrect it. It may not be quite as good as the original, but who can duplicate a child's idea of divinity?

My recipe tester, Hunter Lewis, stole a version of this cake from his North Carolina grandmother.

Cake

- 1¼ cups cake flour
- 1½ cups sugar
- 13 large egg whites, at room temperature
- 1½ teaspoons cream of tartar
- Pinch of salt
- 3 tablespoons honey or molasses
- 1 tablespoon vanilla extract

Toffee crunch

- 1 cup sugar
- 1 cup packed light brown sugar
- 1 teaspoon baking soda

Icing

- ½ cup brewed espresso
- 2 large egg yolks
- ¼ cup sugar
- 8 tablespoons (1 stick) unsalted butter, at room temperature

Confectioners' sugar, for dusting

MAKE THE CAKE

Heat the oven to 350 degrees.

Sift the cake flour and ½ cup of the sugar into a bowl. Set aside.

In a large bowl, whip the egg whites with an electric mixer until foamy. Add the cream of tartar and continue to whip until soft peaks form. Slowly add the remaining 1 cup sugar, about 2 tablespoons at a time, and continue to whip until medium peaks form. Gradually fold the flour and sugar mixture and salt into the egg whites. Fold in the honey or molasses and vanilla.

Transfer the batter to an ungreased angel food cake pan. Bake for 35 to 45 minutes, or until a skewer inserted near the center comes out dry.

Invert the pan and let cool completely upside down (invert the pan onto a long-necked bottle if your pan doesn't have feet), about 1 hour.

MAKE THE TOFFEE CRUNCH

Oil a baking sheet. Combine the sugar, brown sugar, and 1 cup water in a heavy stainless steel saucepan and cook over medium-high heat, stirring, until the sugar dissolves. Then cook, without stirring, until the caramel becomes a deep amber color, 6 to 8 minutes. Remove from the heat and carefully add the baking soda, which will foam. Pour the toffee onto the baking sheet and let cool.

MAKE THE ICING

Combine the espresso, egg yolks, and sugar in the top of a double boiler or in a small heatproof bowl set over a saucepan of simmering water and cook, whisking, until thickened. Let cool.

In a medium bowl, beat the butter with an electric mixer until smooth. Blend in the cooled espresso mixture.

ASSEMBLE THE CAKE

Break the toffee into bite-sized pieces.

Run a knife around the sides of the cake pan and the center tube and unmold the cake. Slice into 3 horizontal layers. Spread one quarter of the icing on the bottom layer and sprinkle with one third of the toffee pieces. Lay the second cake layer on top and repeat, spreading with one quarter of the icing and sprinkling with one third of the toffee. Top with the final cake layer. Ice the cake with the remaining frosting and dot with the remaining pieces of toffee. Dust with the confectioners' sugar and serve. Store in the refrigerator if not serving right away.

INDEX

Page numbers in *italics* refer to photographs.

chicken breasts with poblano chiles, 142–43

duck liver and potato salad with chile vinaigrette, 29–30, *31*

garden salad, 72

lobster and potato chip salad, 86–88, *87*

pancetta, and poached egg salad, 81

perfect roast chicken with mashed potatoes and spinach, 148–49

sesame-crusted goat cheese cakes on, 75–77, *76*

turkey breast Milanese, 152–53

warm dandelion, bacon, and potato salad, 82–83

warm squid salad, 84–85

wild mushroom salad, 78–80

wilted, and goat cheese sandwich, 100

grilling tips, 8–9

Gruyère and bacon burger with guacamole, 112–13

guacamole

bacon and Gruyère burger with, 112–13

and fresh chips, 19

warm lobster tacos with, *230*, 231–32

H

ham

prosciutto and Fontina sandwich, grilled, 110

smoked, and cabbage, lasagna with, 136–37

hazelnuts and oranges, asparagus with, *24*, *25*

herbs, in bouquet garni, 5

Hubbard squash

late-autumn vegetable casserole, 247

huckleberries or blueberries, brined pork loin with, 176–77

J

johnnycakes, goat cheese, 190–93, *192*

K

knives, 9

L

lamb

shoulder, braised, with fried shallots, 186–87

T-bones and eggplant, *184*, 185

temperature, prior to cooking, 7

lasagna with smoked ham and cabbage, 136–37

leek(s)

and roasted peanuts, sautéed shrimp with, 222–24, *223*

and wild mushroom soup, 61

lemon-lime meringue pie, 267–68, *268*

lime-lemon meringue pie, 267–68, *268*

linguine with soft-shell crabs, 129

liver

chicken, and apple mousse, 27–28

duck, and potato salad with chile vinaigrette, 29–30, *31*

lobster

broiled, with zucchini and chile butter, 233

and potato chip salad, 86–88, *87*

salad sandwich, 106

tacos, warm, with guacamole, *230*, 231–32

thermidor, 234

and tomato bisque, 66–67, *67*

roasted, seared steak, and onion rings, 44–47, *45*

sweet, sea scallops on, 225

sweet, tart, warm, 22–23

types of, 9–10

Vidalia, and sweet corn soup, *58, 59*

orange(s)

and hazelnuts, asparagus with, *24, 25*

sauce, blood, grilled swordfish with, 214–15, *215*

organic ingredients, buying, 10

oyster(s)

hot, with black pepper butter, 41

stuffing, pheasant with, 161–63, *162*

P

pancakes

goat cheese johnnycakes, 190–93, *192*

red pepper, with corn and caviar, 16–18, *17*

pancetta, greens, and poached egg salad, 81

Parmesan, bacon, scallions, and tomato, pizza with, 116–17, *117*

pasta

with asparagus, 128

fettuccine, sea scallop, 130–31

fettuccine with calamari and summer squash, *134, 135*

fettuccine with cremini mushrooms and onion marmalade, 126–27, *127*

lasagna with smoked ham and cabbage, 136–37

linguine with soft-shell crabs, 129

spaghetti, whole wheat, with spicy clams, *132, 133*

tagliatelle with beets and cream, *123,* 124–25

pastry crust, my, 266

peanut(s)

-chile sauce, tuna with, 208–9

roasted, and leeks, sautéed shrimp with, 222–24, *223*

pear(s)

-apple crisp, 260

poached in Beaujolais, 264

peas

brick chicken with rosé wine, bacon, and, 146–47

salmon with roasted garlic cream, 202–4, *203*

spicy, soft-shell crab with, 235

pepper(s). *See also* chile(s)

butter, roasted red, corn with, 250

crispy chicken and goat cheese burritos, 48–49

eggplant, zucchini, and pesto sandwich, 114–15

lobster salad sandwich, 106

and onions, mixed, 248

pancakes, red, with corn and caviar, 16–18, *17*

-potato gratin, filet mignon with, 172–73

restaurant-style vegetables, 246

roasted, and eggplant soup, chilled, 54–55

tuna steaks with ginger–black pepper sauce, 206–7

pesto, 114

pheasant with oyster stuffing, 161–63, *162*

pie, lemon-lime meringue, 267–68, *268*